the
YOUNG THAILAND
cookbook

the
YOUNG THAILAND
cookbook

Wandee Young &
Byron Ayanoglu

RANDOM HOUSE OF CANADA

Published in 1995 by Random House of Canada Limited, Toronto.

Canadian Cataloguing in Publication Data

Young, Wandee
The Young Thailand cookbook

Includes index.
ISBN 0-394-22452-3

1. Cookery, Thai.   I. Ayanoglu, Byron.   II. Title.
III. Title: Thailand cookbook.

TX724.5.T5Y65   1995   641.59593   C95-931180-7

Book design: Sharon Foster Design
Cover and interior illustrations: Susan Todd

Printed and bound in Canada

To Pion Saelow with love

❧

"As long as there are fish in the water
and rice in the fields the people are happy."
—THAI PROVERB

Great Thanks to:

Mary Adachi
  the best editor in Canada

Douglas Pepper
  publisher/star-maker

Martha Reilly
  and her masterly word-processing

Andreas Achaz
  of The Regent Hotel, Bangkok

Moynee Wongwatkit Chorthip

Algis Kemezys

Ketsaraporn Ketchulame
  of the Regent Hotel, Bangkok

Diane Martin

Nualpan Osthananda
  of The Oriental Hotel, Bangkok

Kirati Saingam
  of The Landmark Hotel, Bangkok

Dang Buncha Saobuppha

Vinka Valentine

Catherine Yolles

and all the excellent people of
  the Young Thailand *restaurants*

Contents

Introduction

THE CHEF: WANDEE YOUNG

The history of Thai food in Canada is very closely aligned to the life and cooking of a remarkable woman, my co-author, Wandee Young. Born Wandee Saelow in Phuket (south-western Thailand), to a foodie family, she grew up in Bangkok, where her farming parents relocated to open an eatery and join the modern world. She worked alongside her mother, Pion Saelow, who taught the enterprising Wandee everything she knows, not only in the kitchen, but also in the office, in running the business and making it survive.

These were skills that would come in extremely handy years later, when at the age of thirty-five, Wandee found herself an immigrant in the decidedly new-world surroundings of Toronto, Canada. With neither money nor language, and the necessity of caring for her young son, Seksarn, she took on the meanest kind of kitchen employment.

At a stage in life when most people who come from middle-class backgrounds expect some kind of comfort and security, Wandee was taking out the garbage and skinning endless chickens, for something like $1.50 an hour. In so doing, she joined many other aspiring first-worlders, who arrive dazed and needy, but willing to do almost anything to get a foothold in the new economy.

Within a year, Wandee had miraculously scraped together enough money to open a restaurant. That was in 1980, a time when there was not a single Thai restaurant in all of Canada. Her place, built into an ugly, Eglinton Avenue ex-greasy spoon, was called YOUNG THAILAND.

This venture lasted less than one year. (The lack of capital, the unglamorous venue, and most of all, Wandee's need to devote time to her son contributed to its demise.) But it marked the start of what has now become a flood of Thai restaurants in this country and the beginning of Wandee's impressive ambassadorship of her native cuisine.

The restaurant was open just long enough for the true aficionados of faraway cuisines to discover her. Among those instant Thai-food converts was Patty Habib, who was about to open an entertainment palace with a Caribbean theme called The Bamboo. Patty invited the newly unemployed Wandee to head the kitchens, where she proceeded to work out an eclectically fused menu of Caribbean and Thai specialties. A "kalaloo soup meets *pad Thai*" sort of mix that blended the sun-belt culinary elements of two regions on opposite sides of the globe, but with similar climates and topographies, and a taste for hot and perky cooking.

The imaginative menu and spectacularly caring and supportive collaboration between Patty and Wandee lasted for seven years, during which time The Bamboo became an institution on the firmament of Toronto's newly embraced *joie-de-vivre*, and Wandee Young, a name synonymous with Thai cooking.

By the end of the affluent eighties, Wandee scrimped and saved enough money to try her hand at business again. Much more grounded now, her son already a teenager, and with a budget just this side of "shoestring", she settled on an eight-step walk-up, ex-student cafeteria near Ryerson Polytechnic University—another "challenging" location, but by now Wandee is unstoppable. Her legion of fans from The Bamboo descend on her, and devour everything she cooks.

Almost fifty Thai restaurants have opened in Toronto since the Gerrard Street YOUNG THAILAND was created in 1990. By coincidence, the chefs (and

chef-owners) of the best ones are trainees and ex-sous chefs of Wandee Young. Happily there seems to be an inexhaustible source of clients for all of them, including Wandee's biggest YOUNG THAILAND yet, a rambling, bright, party-like space on Church Street, which she opened in 1993. The two YOUNG THAILANDS, minutes from each other in the heart of Toronto's downtown, serve about six hundred happy clients a day, seven days a week. That makes 219,000 a year, and trust me, every single one of them is guaranteed to return for more *pad Thai* and spring rolls, fiery-yet-comforting soups, stews and other lovely things.

Now that we've discovered Thai food, we won't let it go. Our surroundings are not exactly tropical—not even close—but we can allow ourselves to be transported to the palm-fringed coves of the Andaman Sea, with its long hot days and night breezes, just by indulging in its cuisine.

Here, now, Wandee's Thai cooking, demystified. Herein all her secrets, and all her expertise, adapted to the Canadian marketplace and subtly modified for the Canadian sensibility: less oil, minimum salt and "just enough" chili.

Bon Appetit.

BYRON AYANOGLU
Toronto, 1995

Thai Cooking: Hot and Lively

Most Thai cooking happens in the wok. Tossing, folding, stirring, stir-frying allows the foodstuffs only brief, searing contact with heat and results in varying textures and natural tastes. It is a cooking of speedy, almost nervous hand movements, with one or even two wok-shovels (smoothly curved spatulas) working simultaneously, preventing overcooking, anticipating the end which always arrives sooner than one (who is used to western cooking) could possibly expect.

What is even more surprising about Thai food is that it addresses all four of the palate's principal taste elements simultaneously. Bitter (chilies), salty (soya sauce, fish sauce), sweet (sugar, fruits, sweet peppers) and sour (vinegar, lime juice, tamarind), they find their way into every sauce and explode the taste buds. It is the only cuisine of which I'm aware that manages to do this so very successfully, and it is this very characteristic, this assault on the entirety of one's tasting faculties, that we find so irresistible. There is literally no rest from enjoyment when indulging in this cuisine: no margin for jadedness.

Having secured our sense of taste, Thai cooks turn their attention to our sense of smell. Perfumes and scents—basil, coriander, lime leaf, garlic, lemon grass, ginger and galangal, cumin seed, turmeric, coconut—combine and recombine in subtle variations, in dizzying, exhilarating and lusty flavours that one remembers long after the meal has been digested.

As if all that were not enough reason to love Thai cookery, there is also the eye appeal. I have yet to be presented with a Thai dish that I didn't immediately crave. Richly coloured, and simply garnished, every plate is an edible work of art, and it comes naturally. There are no overwrought haute-cuisine style accoutrements here. The beauty of the final presentation is inherent in the specific combinations of the ingredients and the vibrant, satin-smooth sauces that happen effortlessly in the wok. Once the cooking is over, one simply transfers the dish onto a serving plate and more often than not, the only garnishes are the ubiquitous coriander leaves and thin strips of red pepper.

The recipes Wandee has chosen for this book include precious little deep-frying because both she and I feel that home-frying is annoying and wasteful: it smells up the house and requires far too much oil. We have, instead, concentrated on the stir-fried specialties, which divide themselves neatly into two categories: the oil-based and the coconut milk-based.

Oil-based cooking always starts with stir-fried garlic and proceeds with additional spices and flavourings, alongside the main ingredients of vegetables with either fish, seafood or meat. It never requires more than 5-7 minutes of total cooking and usually employs a bit of cornstarch at the end to bind its sauce.

Coconut milk sauces involve the use of curry pastes (either the moderate "red" or the fiery "green") and need a few minutes of advance boiling in order to coax the oil of the coconut milk itself to appear and give the final result its characteristic, shiny look. (Conversely, in coconut milk-based soups, the liquid is never allowed to reach a boil so that the oil stays bound in the coconut and does not form an oily film on the soup).

The one ingredient that crosses over all Thai cooking seems to be *nam pla*, fish sauce. This salty, pungent, soya sauce-like condiment is as essential to the Thai taste as salt and pepper are to western food. Its salt content is obviously its main attraction, but its essence of the sea (derived from squid or other fishy creatures) that smells so strong before cooking, spreads in the sauces, and gives them definition and Thai authenticity.

The other staple is a liberal use of fresh coriander leaves and the thinly sliced sweet pepper strips that top everything from salads to deeply flavoured curries.

Some Helpful Hints

Wok vs. frying pan: no contest. Thai food is best prepared in a wok. I have, however, allowed for a frying pan to be used instead, as long as the cook is prepared to face an important difference: the frying pan has a larger cooking surface than a wok. Things will therefore cook faster in it, and liquids will reduce more readily, which means that brisker stir-frying is necessary, and less time needed to stir-fry garlic (20 seconds instead of 30), or bring coconut milk to readiness (1½ minutes, not 2).

Gas stove vs. electric: again, no contest. "Cooking with gas" is being on the right track, whenever one needs to reduce heat in a hurry, as often happens in these recipes. If one must use electric, it is prudent to employ two elements at once—one at high and the other at medium—and move the wok from one to the other, as the occasion warrants.

Timing: almost everything in this book needs to be "served immediately". So how is that possible with a multi-course meal? The trick is in the preparation. Do all your chopping, slicing and measuring ahead of time, and cook the rice just before the meal begins. Then make a quick soup and/or a salad and start the meal. When the soup/salad are eaten, return to the kitchen, stir-fry and come back to the table with the warm rice and the newly created, piping hot dish (or two) for the main course.

Chopping/slicing: a sharp chef's knife with a heavy handle and a sure stroke is the second most important piece of equipment one needs after a wok. There is a lot of fine-chopping and thin-slicing going on, as well as mincing of things like garlic and "rough-chopping" of onion (cutting it up to roughly ½-inch/ 1-cm pieces, that need not be uniform in size).

Processed vs. fresh: obviously fresh or home-made is always to be preferred. However, we in Canada have neither the time nor the availability that one finds in Thailand. Luckily, we have a healthy economy that allows us to import whatever we wish. All major centres in this country boast markets (usually pan-Asian) which are well-stocked with the most labour-intensive and authentic Thai ingredients.

Curry pastes in cans; bamboo shoots in jars or cans (and already thinly sliced for instant use); a full range of bottled fish sauces, soya sauces and hot sauces; fresh tropical fruits; lemon grass, galangal root, long green beans and eggplants, lime leaves (in three versions: fresh, frozen and dried); packaged black fungus and dried shiitake; and a whole range of fresh fish and frozen, pre-cleaned seafood (which loses very little of taste or texture for having been frozen, with the proviso that shrimps should be purchased shell-on, and shelled at home after thawing, for best texture).

Speaking of ingredients, here follows a list of the unusual items used in this book.

CONDIMENTS AND SAUCES

Chilies: come in many forms and in prepared sauces. Rumour has it that it was the Portuguese who introduced chilies to Thailand in the not-too-distant past, but Thai cuisine deploys them as if they've had them forever. In this book we use the thin, small variety that can be purchased fresh from Asian stores and always has some green and some red specimens. In the recipes these chilies are called "hot, fresh chilies". The same chilies, when they're dried in the sun, turn all red and can be found, whole or crushed, in most stores and supermarkets. We have used the dry ones to make "Roasted Chilies".

Chili-garlic sauce: an invention of Vietnam is a mixture of chilies, garlic and vinegar. It is quite hot and comes pre-mixed in a jar. It has a long life.

Chili paste: also pre-mixed and has a long life. It is slightly less hot, and mixed with soya bean oil.

Coconut milk: must be of the unsweetened variety. It is not homogenized and one finds the fatty solids separated from the liquid. When using one cup at a time, take some solids and some liquid. The two blend into a cream the moment they are heated and stirred in the wok. By the time the rest of the can (the second cup) is added, the solid-liquid content will be balanced out.

Curry pastes: multi-ingredient condiments that form the essential tastes of Thai curries and stews. They can be home-made, but there is no need, since excellent versions can be purchased canned and ready to use. The unused portion should be frozen until the next occasion. There are at least six types of curry paste in Thai cooking, but we use only three:

    Red curry paste, the most common, is hot and lusty, a reddish-brown colour. It uses red dried chilies, with garlic, aromatics and spices, as well as shrimp paste.

    Green curry paste is extremely hot, being based on fresh, green chilies, with similar additions to its "red" cousin.

    Masaman curry paste has friendlier heat, employing less chilies and additional sweet spices. It is used in making the addictively delicious masaman beef curry.

Fish sauce (Nam pla): a dark sauce of salt with essence of fish or squid, it has a strong taste that blends in beautifully with all other Thai condiments. It must be used judiciously for the Canadian palate, even though in Thailand people sprinkle it liberally into dishes that already have lots of it. It is also the prime ingredient of Thai cuisine's most popular hot sauce, meant to be served on the side of any and all dishes (see Young Thailand Hot Sauce).

Galangal root: a relative of ginger root. It is a slightly bitter, highly aromatic ingredient that can be found more and more readily in Canada. It is used unpeeled and sliced in rounds, mostly in soups. It remains hard to chew after cooking, but is left in the soup to continue its flavour-giving. If unable to locate it, one can substitute ginger root, though at a loss of authenticity.

Lemon grass: another hard-to-chew aromatic. This is a woody and slender weed that imparts an indispensible lemony taste. It is available in Asian stores and some supermarkets. To use it, one must first break it up with one smash of the flat side of a chef's knife. It is then usually sliced in 1-inch/2.5-cm pieces. Although it is left in in the final presentation, it is to be avoided when eating.

Lime leaf: a wondrously limey condiment from the Kaffir lime tree. It is normally used in chunks (leaves torn into thirds or quarters) and is as hard to chew as galangal or lemon grass, though it too is left in the dishes and soups that use it. In occasional recipes it is shredded very finely and in that form it becomes edible. Lime leaves are now available fresh and frozen and both kinds must be washed before use. It is also possible to find dried lime leaves, which come back to usable shape after a 20-minute soak in cold water. If unable to find lime leaf in any shape or form, then one can (very inadequately) replace it with 1 tbsp/15 mL of lime juice per leaf.

Sesame oil: a dark-brown, syrupy oil of Chinese descent. It has a thick sesame taste and is used sparingly for its flavour.

Shrimps: in demand for many of Wandee's recipes in their fresh form, but we also offer uses for two processed varieties:

    Dried shrimps: preserved in salt and used for their pungent, fishy contribution to otherwise sweet dishes.

    Shrimp paste: lends taste similar to dried shrimps except that it can blend and melt into liquids and is used to suffuse sauces that require its characteristic flavours. It is a staple ingredient of all curry pastes.

Soya sauce: has wide-ranging uses in Thai cooking, mostly for its salt. Wandee often uses it instead of fish sauce when changing a recipe to suit vegetarians. She also uses it alongside fish sauce when additional salt is needed, without having to overdo the strong taste of the fish sauce. We recommend the earthy taste of Chinese soya sauce, instead of the more refined Japanese variety, or the sweetness of tamari. (Though, obviously, this is a matter of taste). There are three other soya derivatives that are encountered in this book:

    Dark soya sauce: a syrupy version that is sweetened with molasses, and is particularly effective in marinades.

    Oyster sauce: a soya sauce bolstered with oyster extract, sugar and thickener, for more robust sauces.

    Salted soya beans: for a sweet and meaningful soya content used in particular recipes. These come in a long-life jar, imported from Singapore, and resemble baked beans in a clear sauce. They are light brown in colour.

Spicy rice: an idiosyncratic Thai ingredient that doesn't taste of much and adds a gritty textural subtext to Thai ground meat salads, themselves an acquired taste. It can be made at home by baking raw rice till brown, and then grinding it to fine meal in a coffee grinder or blender; or it can be bought ready-made. We have included it in the "ingredients" list of dishes that call for it, but marked it "optional". Test it on a small quantity of the recipe before using it.

Tamarind: a sweet and sour fruit that adds a fruity tartness to a number of favourite Thai recipes, including *Pad Thai*. It is the juice that is used, derived by diluting concentrated tamarind pulp with warm water and mashing it through a strainer to render a muddy, thick syrup. The pulp (also known as "tamarind paste") is available in all Asian stores. Leftovers can be covered and refrigerated for a long time.

Tomato paste: diluted in water appears in several recipes of this book, especially the "sweet and sour" creations. It is used mostly for its colour and somewhat for its tomato flavour. Don't tell anyone I told you, but it is entirely possible to substitute plain old ketchup, using about 2 tbsp/25 mL of it, where the recipe calls for ½ tsp/2 mL tomato paste dissolved in 1 tbsp/15 mL water.

Vinegar: an important ingredient of Thai side sauces, as well as the gravies of certain stews, particularly the "sweet and sour" varieties. White vinegar serves, but for a more refined taste try a Chinese or Japanese rice vinegar.

Vegetables

Bamboo shoots: sold in cans and jars, as well as in bulk out of plastic tubs. Most Thai recipes call for bamboo shoots in strips, and it is possible to buy them already sliced. It is important to wash and drain them to eliminate the processing odours.

Basil: the most aromatic of all herbs is a favourite of Thai cooking. The Italian variety serves, but the one found in Asian markets is tastier and a little bit bitter. Most of our recipes call for "20 leaves", but this is a generic figure. One usually needs about half or a third of a bundle, depending on its size, and using more than exactly 20 leaves never hurt any dish.

Black fungus: sounds like some kind of medieval pestilence but is actually a mushroomy growth on tree trunks (it is also known as "tree-ear") that is available dried. When it is soaked in cold water, it swells to many times its original size and one ounce of the dry product becomes enough for a soup of 4 servings. It doesn't taste of much, but it has a delightful crunchy texture.

Coriander (or cilantro): the parsley-like fresh herb that is no longer an oddity for modern foodies. No cuisine (not even Mexican) uses it as much as Thai. It goes into a number of sauces and becomes the final garnish of absolutely every dish.

Eggplant: the purple-skinned, white-fleshed, spongy wonder-substance that loves being cooked in oil. The type we recommend is the long, thin Asian variety that needs less ado than the fatter, regular eggplants, and has a light purple skin that turns a gorgeous lapis lazuli when cooked.

Long green beans: about a foot long and a little less green than ordinary green beans. Both ends must be trimmed of hard stems before use. They can be found in all Asian stores and in some supermarkets.

Red bell pepper: the second most common vegetable in Thai cooking (after coriander). Its sweet, brightly coloured flesh finds its way into a lot of dishes, either in square chunks or in thin strips, and as finely sliced strips, always as a final garnish (along with coriander).

Shiitake mushrooms: commonly found in dried form. It sounds expensive at first but one usually needs a tiny quantity (half an ounce for a dish of 4 servings). Shiitake must be soaked in hot water for 20 minutes, until they swell to many times their original size, and become soft enough to stir-fry for a few minutes and turn into earthy, meaty wonderfulness.

Tofu

Fresh, pressed tofu: comes in 4-inch/10-cm square cakes and is used in curries and vegetarian dishes.

Fried tofu: pressed tofu that has been fried. It can be prepared at home by ambitious chefs, by frying pressed tofu in vegetable oil.

Soft tofu: packed in water and is used in soups.

Noodles

Rice Sticks: the most common Thai noodle is flat, about 1/8 inch/2.5 mm thick and opaque, like a faded linguine. It is a magical substance, in that it does most of its "cooking" when soaked in cold water (for 1-24 hours). When ready to use it, one simply drains it, and boils it (for less than a minute) or refries it for 2-3 minutes, for an *al dente*, slightly slippery, highly satisfying texture.

Thin rice sticks (vermicelli): thinner by half than its cousin, it needs less soaking (15 minutes only) and less cooking, for a lovely texture and slurping pleasure.

Bean threads (glass noodles): a true miracle of culinary technology, this mung bean derivative comes in packages of 8 detachable portions. It needs about 1 hour of soaking in cold water, until it swells to many times its original volume and then cooks up in no time. It works in soups as well as noodle dishes.

Rice

The staff of Thai life, rice is served at every meal, and every main-course dish is designed to go with it. Any rice of one's preference can be steamed to accompany Thai dishes, but the most suitable comes from Thailand, and the best thereof is called Jasmin Rice.

Sticky rice: used for Thai sweets. Avoid the Japanese variety which is too chewy, and use the Thai (specifically the one called Peacock Extra-Super Quality) which cooks soft and moist: ideal for desserts.

Spring Roll Skins

For frying: they come in packages of 10 or 20, and in various sizes. Wandee prefers the large square kind rather than the smaller round ones because they wrap more neatly, thus preventing leaks during frying. They are soft and cream coloured. Wrap leftovers tightly and store in the cold to avoid drying out.

For steaming: rice-paper sheets. These are hard, thin, plastic-like sheets that require a quick pass through boiled water to soften them. They are used for cold spring rolls. Leftovers can be stored in their original package and kept in the larder.

OK, that's it. Let's cook.

APPETIZERS

Chicken Satay

1 lb	skinless, boneless chicken breast	500 g
	MARINADE:	
1 tsp	black pepper	5 mL
1 tsp	ground cumin	5 mL
1 tsp	ground coriander	5 mL
1/2 tsp	tumeric	2 mL
1 tsp	chopped garlic	5 mL
1 tbsp	sugar	15 mL
1 tbsp	vegetable oil	15 mL
1 tbsp	soya sauce	15 mL
1 tbsp	lemon juice	15 mL
1 tsp	fish sauce	5 mL
16	bamboo skewers	16

A little oil or coconut milk
Peanut Sauce
Fresh coriander leaves
Lettuce leaves

Serves 4

Marinated and skewered meat slow-charred on gently glowing embers has a universal ability to unleash appetite, and satay is the skewer of choice in all of Southeast Asia. This version uses chicken (although pork can easily be substituted). Wandee makes it her own, lavishing as many flavours on its marinade as she does on the famous Peanut Sauce that is meant to accompany it.

1. Cut thin (1/4-inch/5-mm) slices that run the length of the chicken breast (each slice will be 1 inch x 4 inches x 1/4 inch/ 2.5 cm x 10 cm x 5 mm approximately) to get 16 slices. If you find it difficult to cut thinly through fresh meat, leave it in the freezer for 15-20 minutes to harden slightly and then slice.

2. Place the chicken strips in a work bowl. Add all the marinating ingredients (solids first, then the liquids) and gently toss until well mixed. Let the chicken marinate in the fridge for at least 2 hours and up to 24.

3. When ready to cook the satays, stir chicken in its marinade and then thread each slice onto a skewer, working the skewer in and out of the meat, down the middle of the slice, so that it stays in place during grilling.

4. Baste the chicken with oil or coconut milk and grill on a barbecue (that has been burning for a while and is no longer scorching hot) or under the broiler of an indoor oven. Cook for not much more than 2 minutes each side, turning fairly often to prevent unnecessary burning, and baste one more time with oil or coconut milk. The satays are done when they have turned golden brown and crispy along the edges.

5. Serve on lettuce leaves, decorated with fresh coriander leaves, and accompanied by a small bowl of Peanut Sauce *(page 36)* on the side.

Lamb Satay

Same idea as the Chicken Satay, except that this one uses lamb, which has plenty of flavour of its own and thus needs less spicing.

1. Cut the lamb into thin (¼-inch/5-mm) slices that are 1 inch x 4 inches x ¼ inch/2.5 cm x 10 cm x 5 mm. If some pieces are not quite as long as needed, not to worry: you will be able to use two smaller pieces to make up the skewers. If you find it difficult to cut thinly through fresh meat, leave it in the freezer for 15-20 minutes to harden slightly and then slice.

2. Place the lamb strips in a work bowl. Add the garlic, pepper, sugar, soya sauce and oil and toss gently to coat thoroughly. Add the lemon juice and dark soya sauce and toss again. Let the lamb marinate in the fridge for at least 2 hours and up to 24.

3. When ready to cook the satays, thread the strips onto skewers, working the skewers in and out of the meat, down the middle of the slices, so that they stay in place during the grilling.

4. Baste generously with the excess marinade and grill on a barbecue (that has been burning for a while and is no longer scorching hot) or under the broiler of an indoor oven. Cook for not much more than 2 minutes each side, turning fairly often to prevent unnecessary burning, and baste once again with the marinating juices. The satays are done when they have charred along the edges and have turned shiny and dark (from the dark soya sauce).

5. Serve on lettuce leaves, decorated with fresh coriander leaves, and accompanied by a small bowl of Peanut Sauce *(page 36)* on the side.

1 lb	trimmed lamb from shoulder or leg	500 g
	Marinade:	
1 tsp	chopped garlic	5 mL
1 tsp	black pepper	5 mL
1 tbsp	sugar	15 mL
3 tbsp	soya sauce	45 mL
1 tbsp	vegetable oil	15 mL
1 tbsp	lemon juice	15 mL
1 tsp	dark soya sauce	5 mL
16	bamboo skewers	16
	Peanut Sauce	
	Fresh coriander leaves	
	Lettuce leaves	

Serves 4

Thai Chicken Wings

8	chicken wings	8
	MARINADE:	
1 tsp	black pepper	5 mL
1 tsp	ground ginger	5 mL
1 tbsp	chopped garlic	15 mL
1 tsp	sugar	5 mL
1 tbsp	soya sauce	15 mL
2 tbsp	oyster sauce	25 mL
2 tbsp	vegetable oil	25 mL
2 tbsp	lemon juice	25 mL
1-2 tbsp	chili-garlic sauce (or cayenne)	15-25 mL

YOUNG THAILAND Hot Sauce
Thai Sweet and Sour Sauce
Cucumber Salad
Fresh coriander leaves

Serves 4.

The once humble wings are now flying all over the place, costing as much at the butcher's as the chicken's more worthwhile parts. They do, however, make a delightful appetizer and Wandee has responded to popular taste with this high-voltage recipe.

1. Cut off the thin arm of the wing and save for stock-making. Separate the remaining wing into its two parts by cutting at the joint. Repeat with all 8 wings, to end up with 16 pieces. Place wing pieces in a work bowl and add all the marinade ingredients. Toss and stir to blend well. Let rest in the refrigerator for at least 2 hours and up to 24.
2. When ready to bake the wings, preheat oven to 400° F/200° C. Roll the wings in the marinade and then transfer to a baking sheet. Bake for 25-30 minutes, turning them after 15 minutes and basting with the leftover marinade. Take them out when they are shiny and golden brown with some crisp edges.
3. Serve immediately, topped with some fresh coriander leaves, and accompanied by Thai Sweet and Sour Sauce *(page 38)* and YOUNG THAILAND Hot Sauce *(page 37)*, as well as the Cucumber Salad *(page 23)*.

Cucumber Salad

A simply dressed and refreshing idea for cucumber, this salad balances the furious heat of most things Thai and is very useful on the side of a number of the dishes in this book.

1. Wash and dry cucumber. (Peel the cucumber if not using English.) Cut in half lengthwise and then into quarters. Slice the quarters into ¼-inch/5-mm pieces. Arrange on a plate.
2. Thinly slice juliennes of red pepper and red onion. Scatter on the cucumber decoratively.
3. In a small bowl whisk sugar, vinegar and salt, until well mixed. Distribute this dressing evenly over the vegetables and top generously with fresh coriander leaves.

10 inches	cucumber (preferably English)	25 cm
½	small red onion	½
⅓	medium red pepper	⅓
1 tbsp	sugar	15 mL
2 tbsp	rice (or white) vinegar	25 mL
½ tsp	salt	2 mL

Fresh coriander leaves

Serves 4.

Spring Rolls

Filling:

1½ oz	glass noodles	45 g
½ oz	dry black fungus	15 g
¼ cup	shredded white cabbage	50 mL
½ cup	bamboo shoot strips	125 mL
1	small white onion, thinly sliced	1
¼ cup	grated carrot	50 mL
3	stems green onion, in ½-inch/1-cm pieces	3
4 oz	skinless, boneless chicken breast	125 g
½ cup	vegetable oil	125 mL
1 tbsp	chopped garlic	15 mL
1 tsp	black pepper	5 mL
1 tbsp	sugar	15 mL
1 tbsp	soya sauce	15 mL
1 tsp	fish sauce	5 mL
1 tbsp	oyster sauce	15 mL

The ultimate deep-fried thrill—better than fries, even more addictive than Southern chicken—is indisputably the Southeast Asian spring roll. Crispy and light on the outside, flavourful, toothsome and mysterious inside, this is sinful self-indulging at its most forgivable: how can anyone be faulted for craving it; how can anyone resist eating it? The best news is that, despite all the oil that this recipe calls for, very little of it ends up in the spring roll itself.

The version described here is the classic spring roll that one can find everywhere, from Bangkok to the Muskokas. Wandee has concocted three additional versions, which are noted at the end of the recipe.

There are three phases to spring-roll heaven: the filling, rolling and frying.

1. The long list of filling ingredients are stir-fried in a wok or frying pan, added one by one in dizzyingly quick intervals. It is therefore essential that the various items be prepared and reserved, ready to be used. Begin by separately soaking the glass noodles and the dry black fungus in cold water (for at least 30 minutes).

2. Prepare the shredded cabbage, bamboo shoot strips, sliced onion, grated carrot and chopped green onion. Reserve these ingredients separately.

3. Pound and chop chicken breast with a chef's knife until it is minced. Reserve.

4. Now return to the glass noodles, drain and reserve them. Also drain the black fungus (it will have swollen to 5-6 times its original size and become shiny and slightly slippery), wash it several times in running cold water, drain and reserve.

5. Heat ½ cup/125 mL of oil in a wok (or frying pan) on high heat. Add the chopped garlic and stir-fry for 30 seconds. Add the black pepper and stir-fry for another 30 seconds. Add the minced chicken, stir-frying for 1 minute until the strands have separated.

6. Lower the fire and in quick succession, stirring after each addition, add bamboo shoots, black fungus, sugar, soya sauce, fish sauce, oyster sauce, onions and cabbage (at the same time), the noodles, and carrots with green onions (together), stir-fry everything, tossing and mixing for another minute or so, and then take off the fire.

7. Using a strainer set in a bowl, transfer the contents of the wok into the strainer, so that the oil and other excess liquid of the filling can drain through. Do not press on the mixture, it must drain by itself, and it'll take about 20 minutes (you can use the time to make the Thai Sweet and Sour Sauce that must be served with the spring rolls.)

8. Get ready to roll the spring rolls by mixing the flour and water in a small bowl. This will act as the glue that seals them.

9. Separate a skin (they are approximately 9 inches/22.5 cm square) and lay it out on a dry surface, with one of its points towards you. Place a heaping tablespoon of the stuffing about 2 inches/5 cm in from the point. Fold the point over the stuffing and pull in the stuffing to make it tight. Tuck the flap under the stuffing and roll the skin on it once. Take the triangles of skin that have formed on the two sides and fold them, as if making an envelope. Now you are facing a long rectangle with a point at the bottom end. Roll the stuffed end,

	Skins:	
1 tbsp	flour	15 mL
1 tsp	water	5 mL
8	sheets spring roll skins	8
2½ cups	vegetable oil	625 mL

Thai Sweet and Sour Sauce
Fresh coriander leaves
Fresh lettuce leaves

Serves 4

Thai appetizers can be served anytime during the meal. Various dishes are served in no particular order, since Thai meals are meant to be celebrations of the variety and colourful profusion of the national cuisine.

as tightly as possible, until only the triangle at the bottom is left unrolled. Spread a little of the flour-water paste and then continue rolling to seal it off. You should have a spring roll about 3 inches/7.5 cm long and less than 1 inch/2.5 cm around. Repeat until you have rolled all 8 spring rolls.

10. Heat 2½ cups/625 mL vegetable oil in a wok (or frying pan) over high heat until the oil appears to be moving and threatens to start emitting smoke. Add all 8 spring rolls at once, and fry at high heat for 7-8 minutes, turning once in a while until they have turned golden brown all over. Scoop them out of the oil and stack them standing on their ends to drain excess oil.

11. Cut each roll in half. Serve arranged on lettuce leaves, topped with fresh coriander leaves, and accompanied by dipping bowls of Thai Sweet and Sour Sauce *(page 38)*.

Variations:

Shrimp Spring Rolls I: Peel and devein 8 jumbo shrimps, leaving the tail shell on. Follow exactly the same recipe as above, except that once you have folded the outer flaps of the skin during the rolling process (step #9) place a raw shrimp on the stuffed part, with only its tail sticking out and continue rolling as above. The tail will remain exposed and the body of the shrimp will be rolled inside the skin.

Shrimp Spring Rolls II: Use 4 oz/125 g of cleaned shrimp meat pounded into mince, instead of the chicken in the above recipe, and follow the recipe exactly, stir-frying the shrimp strands instead of the chicken in step #5.

Vegetarian Spring Rolls: *Omit:* chicken, fish sauce and oyster sauce from above recipe. *Replace with:* additional 1½ oz/45 g glass noodles, additional ½ cup/125 mL bamboo shoots, and additional 3 tsp/45 mL soya sauce. Follow the recipe as is, disregarding instructions concerning chicken, fish sauce and oyster sauce, *but* adding the additional noodles, bamboo shoots and soya sauce at the same time as the original amounts of the same are scheduled.

Thai Cold Spring Rolls

8 oz	skinless, boneless chicken breast	250 g
1 cup	bean sprouts	250 mL
1 cup	grated carrot	250 mL
½ tsp	black pepper	2 mL
2 tbsp	sugar	25 mL
3 tbsp	rice (or white) vinegar	45 mL
½ tsp	salt	2 mL
5	egg yolks	5
1 tsp	vegetable oil	5 mL
	Fresh coriander leaves	
4	rice paper sheets	4

This steamed version of spring roll serves double duty: it's a delicious alternative to the fried variety, while being different enough to satisfy in its own right. Furthermore, it is easier to make, fun to eat, a fantasy of splashes of colour inside a delicate white petal. It suffers very little if prepared in advance: an ideal choice for entertaining.

There are four items (plus the ubiquitous coriander leaves) that will be layered to become the filling of the cold spring rolls. They have to be prepared in advance and reserved.

1. Heat 2-3 cups/500-750 mL water to boiling and add the chicken. Poach at high heat for 7-8 minutes, without overcooking. Drain, let cool somewhat and then tear off thin strands by hand. Reserve.
2. Heat 2-3 cups/500-750 mL of water to boiling and add the bean sprouts. Cook on high heat for 30 seconds and drain. They will have become darker, but should still be crunchy. Reserve.
3. Grate carrot through the widest holes of the grater. Transfer to a working bowl and add pepper, sugar, vinegar and salt. Mix well and reserve.
4. Beat the egg yolks lightly. Heat a little oil in a wide frying pan and add the yolks. Cook at medium heat for two minutes: the yolks will quickly jell into a thin, very yellow omelette. Do not overcook (they must not brown), and do not attempt to turn. Slide the cooked omelette carefully onto a cutting board and fold over twice. You will have a three-layered rectangle. Using a sharp knife, thinly slice the omelette lengthwise, creating long juliennes. Reserve.

5. Heat 8-10 cups water/2-2.5 L until hot but not boiling in a wok (or wide pot). Take one of the rice paper sheets (which are round, about 12 inches/30 cm in diameter, thin and stiff) and holding it by one edge, pass it through the water for a second or two. It will become pliable and soft. Grab it by another edge, and moisten the part you were holding earlier. Lay the sheet on a clean work surface and smooth it out.

6. Place a row of chicken shreds (about a quarter of the quantity you have from step #1) running the width of the sheet, a little bit in from the outer edge. Continue layering on this row with the egg juliennes, the marinated carrot shreds, the coriander leaves and the sprouts (about ¼ of each of the ingredients). Flap the outer edge over the stuffing and pull it tight. Roll the spring roll as if it were a long cigar. The final edge will stick to the roll on its own. Repeat with the other 3 sheets. The cold spring rolls are now ready to eat, but can comfortably wait for up to 1½ hours in a dish covered with cling wrap (do not refrigerate, as this would stiffen the rice paper).

7. When ready to serve, cut off a little of the two ends to arrive at the points which are evenly filled. Cut the rest of the spring roll diagonally on the bias in pieces that are 1-1½ inches/2.5-3 cm (you will have 4-5 pieces from each roll). Arrange them on a plate, each piece standing on end and supporting each other, and serve them with Cucumber Salad *(page 23)*, as well as Young Thailand Hot Sauce *(page 37)* or Peanut Sauce *(page 36)* or both.

Cucumber Salad
Young Thailand Hot Sauce and/or
Peanut Sauce

Serves 4.

Variations:

Shrimp Cold Spring Rolls: Clean and devein 8 jumbo shrimps, and boil them in water for only two minutes until white and springy. Julienne them lengthwise, and use two shrimps-worth per spring roll instead of chicken.

Vegetarian Cold Spring Rolls: boil 1 cup/250 mL of bamboo shoot strips for 1 minute and drain. Use them instead of chicken in the recipe.

Stuffed Calamari

Porcelain white squid are stuffed with an aromatic chicken forcemeat. A texture that crackles on the outside and soothes on the inside, this one is for those special occasions when something unusual is called for.

1. To prepare the stuffing, lay the chicken on a cutting board and, using a chef's knife, pound and chop the chicken until finely minced. Transfer to a work bowl. Add all the other stuffing ingredients—onion, green onion, black pepper, soya sauce, garlic, oyster sauce and oil—and mix well to blend.
2. Wash the squid, both the cavities and the exteriors. Stuff each body with as much of the chicken mixture as it will hold.
3. Heat 3 tbsp/45 mL vegetable oil in a wok (or wide frying pan) on high heat, until just about ready to smoke. Add the stuffed squid, reduce the heat to medium-low and cover the wok tightly. Cook for 3 minutes. Uncover to discover the stuffing decoratively bulging out of the squid, which has itself begun to cook and has turned pearly white. Raise the heat to medium-high and fry uncovered for 5-7 minutes, turning several times, until the squid and stuffing are golden brown.
4. Serve immediately on lettuce leaves, topped with fresh coriander leaves, accompanied by Thai Lemon-Coriander Sauce *(page 39)*.

	STUFFING:	
6 oz	skinless, boneless chicken breast	175 g
2 tbsp	finely chopped onion	25 mL
1	stem green onion, chopped	1
½ tsp	black pepper	2 mL
1 tsp	soya sauce	5 mL
1 tsp	chopped garlic	5 mL
½ tsp	oyster sauce	2 mL
1 tsp	vegetable oil	5 mL
12	cleaned squid (8 oz/250 g)	12
3 tbsp	vegetable oil	45 mL
	Lettuce	
	Fresh coriander leaves	
	Thai Lemon-Coriander Sauce	

Serves 4.

Tao Hoo Tod
(Deep-Fried Tofu)

14 oz	fresh, pressed tofu	425 g
1½	cups vegetable oil	375 mL

Lettuce leaves
Fresh coriander leaves
Thai Lemon-Coriander Sauce
Young Thailand Hot Sauce

Serves 4.

Tofu, which sprang into prominence in North America with the alternate life-stylers of the sixties, has been a staple protein in Asia for centuries. Here's an easy recipe of golden crispness that will please both vegetarians and others.

1. Cut tofu cakes into pieces to obtain 12 1½-inch/3-cm squares. Heat the oil in a wok (or wide frying pan) until it is just about to smoke. Add the tofu squares and continue frying at high heat for 3 minutes until golden on the bottom. Turn the tofu and reduce heat to medium-high. Fry this side for 3-5 minutes until also golden (do not overfry, this makes the tofu chewy). Remove tofu from the oil and set on a paper towel to absorb the excess oil.
2. Serve on lettuce leaves, topped with fresh coriander leaves, accompanied by Thai Lemon-Coriander Sauce *(page 39)* and, separately, Young Thailand Hot Sauce *(page 37)*.

Krathong Thong
(Golden Baskets)

❧

Fragile and tiny pastry shells stuffed with an explosively delicate shrimp mixture look spectacular and become easier if you agree to cut a major corner by buying the shells ready-made. Supermarkets carry a selection, but the most suitable and airy are made by Siljans and called "crispy shells". They come in a box of 24, which is how many you'll need for this recipe.

1. Chop/mince shrimps using a chef's knife. Reserve.
2. Finely chop red pepper and onion, combine and reserve.
3. Heat 2 tbsp/25 mL oil in a wok (or frying pan) on medium-high heat. Add chopped garlic and stir-fry for 1 minute. Add minced shrimps and stir-fry for 1 minute. Take the wok off the fire and add soya sauce, sugar, fish sauce and chili-garlic sauce. Stir to mix. Return to the fire and stir-fry for 1 minute. Add reserved onion/red pepper, the peas, chopped coriander and lemon juice and stir-fry 2-3 minutes. Remove from fire and transfer to a work bowl.
4. Working quickly, fill the shells with the stuffing (about 1 tsp/ 5 mL of stuffing per shell). Serve immediately, decorated with fresh coriander leaves.

8	large shrimps, shelled and deveined (5oz/150 g)	8
1	small red pepper	1
1	small onion	1
2 tbsp	vegetable oil	25 mL
1 tsp	chopped garlic	5 mL
1 tbsp	soya sauce	15 mL
1 tsp	sugar	5 mL
1 tbsp	fish sauce	15 mL
½ tsp	chili-garlic sauce	2mL
3 tbsp	green peas (frozen)	45 mL
2 tbsp	chopped coriander	25 mL
1 tbsp	lemon juice	15 mL

24 extra-thin/crispy pastry shells 24
Fresh coriander leaves

Serves 4.

Yum Naem Sod (Ground Pork Salad)

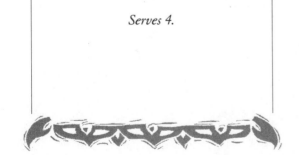

8 oz	pork tenderloin	250 g
3 oz	Thai-style pork rind	90 g
3 tsp	fish sauce	15 mL
3 tbsp	lime juice	45 mL
1/2 tsp	sugar	2 mL
1/2 tsp	roasted chilies	2 mL
1/4	red pepper, julienned	1/4
1 inch	fresh ginger, peeled and julienned	2.5 cm
1	stem green onion, chopped	1
1/2	small red onion, slivered	1/2
2 tbsp	roasted unsalted peanuts	25 mL
2 tbsp	chopped fresh coriander	25 mL

Lettuce leaves
Fresh coriander leaves
Young Thailand Hot Sauce

Serves 4.

A challenging item, this dish presents pork and pork rind in a traditional dressing for a meat salad that Canadians might find bizarre. It does, however, work well in combination with other Thai appetizers, and it is easy to concoct, which makes it a good choice as one of the items on a party buffet. The pork rind that is needed is paper thin and imported from Thailand. The recipe calls for a small quantity, but the rest can be frozen and used in other pork recipes, like pâtés or stews.

1. Slice the pork in long strips and, using a chef's knife, chop/pound until finely minced. Reserve. Also chop the pork rind roughly in 1/2-inch/1-cm bits. Reserve separately.
2. Heat 1/4 cup/50 mL water in a saucepan until boiling. Add pork and stir-boil for 3 minutes, until the bits have come apart. Add pork rind and continue stir-boiling for another 2 minutes. Transfer the meat to a strainer and drain the cooking liquid.
3. Transfer the drained meat to a work bowl and add fish sauce, lime juice, sugar and roasted chilies. Mix well to blend. Add red pepper, fresh ginger, green onion, red onion, peanuts and chopped fresh coriander and mix well.
4. Line a plate with lettuce leaves and heap the pork salad on the lettuce. Top with fresh coriander leaves and serve along with a bowl of Young Thailand Hot Sauce *(page 37)*.

SAUCES AND CONDIMENTS

Peanut Sauce

5 oz	roasted unsalted peanuts	150 g
4 cups	unsweetened coconut milk	1 L
2 tbsp	red curry paste	25 mL
2 tbsp	sugar	25 mL
3 tbsp	lemon juice	45 mL
3 tsp	fish sauce	15 mL

Serves 4 or more.

Maesri, Wandee's favourite brand of red curry paste, comes in 4-oz/112-gm tins. You'll need half a tin per recipe and you can bag and freeze the rest for future use.

Indispensable with satay, this sauce also works as a nice dip for a number of other Asian appetizers (like cold spring rolls) and all kinds of grilled meats. Thinned out with some water, it makes a beautiful salad dressing for sprout salads, like the Indonesian gado-gado. The peanuts that this recipe calls for are widely available. The red curry paste is imported from Thailand.

1. Blend or process the peanuts until they are fine meal. Reserve.
2. Heat half the coconut milk in a saucepan at high heat and add the red curry paste. Stir to dissolve and continue cooking at high heat for 10-12 minutes, until the oil from the coconut has risen to the surface.
3. Lower heat to medium-high and add processed peanuts. Stir and add the rest of the coconut milk. Bring to bubbling boil. Lower heat to medium and add sugar, lemon juice and fish sauce. Cook, stirring occasionally, for 15-20 minutes, until the sauce has thickened somewhat and the oil has returned to the surface.
4. Take off the fire and let rest for a half hour. Stir to blend oil that has risen to the surface. It should be the consistency of thick cream. If thicker than that, add a couple of tablespoons of water or coconut milk and blend.
5. The sauce can be served lukewarm or reheated to piping hot. Leftover sauce can be refrigerated (where it will solidify) and then reheated on a slow fire, thinned down with some water or coconut milk. It can also be frozen, and reheated another day, the same way.

YOUNG THAILAND
Hot Sauce

~⚹~

This is the real thing and must be used with caution. I've seen Thai people dump several tablespoons of it into a single bowl of soup, but that can take some getting used to. This sauce can rightfully accompany (and complement) all Thai dishes.

3 tbsp	lemon or lime juice	45 mL
1 tbsp	chopped garlic	15 mL
3 tbsp	fish sauce	45 mL
1 tbsp	sugar	15 mL
1 tbsp	finely chopped fresh hot chilies (6-7 chilies)	15 mL

too much lime

1. Mix all the ingredients together, stir to dissolve the sugar, let rest for a while, and call the fire department.

Serves 4 or more.

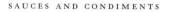

Thai Sweet and Sour Sauce

1 cup	rice (or white) vinegar	250 mL
1 cup	sugar	250 mL
2 tbsp	soya sauce	25 mL
¼ tsp	salt	1 mL
2 tbsp	chili-garlic sauce	25 mL
1 tbsp	chopped garlic	15 mL

Serves 4 or more.

This is a generic sauce that works well with most Thai appetizers and can even be served with soups and grills. It is easy to make in quantity and has a long life.

1. Heat the vinegar and sugar in a saucepan on high heat for 3-4 minutes, until the sugar dissolves. Add soya sauce and salt and stir. Continue cooking at moderately high heat for 10 minutes, until the sauce thickens somewhat. Remove from the fire. Add chili-garlic sauce and the garlic. Stir to blend and let cool. Serve.

THE YOUNG THAILAND COOKBOOK

Thai Lemon-Coriander Sauce

A multi-ingredient sauce that requires no cooking and provides taste without the added fuel of chilies. It can, mind you, serve as an alternate hot sauce, with the simple addition of 1-2 tsp/5-10 mL of Vietnamese chili-garlic sauce stirred in at the end.

1. Thoroughly mix all the ingredients in a work bowl and let rest for 20-30 minutes. Enjoy.

1/2	medium red pepper, finely chopped	1/2
1/2	small red onion, finely chopped	1/2
1 tsp	chopped garlic	5 mL
4 tbsp	soya sauce	50 mL
1 tbsp	vegetable oil	15 mL
1 tbsp	sugar	15 mL
3 tbsp	lemon juice	45 mL
2 tbsp	finely processed roasted unsalted peanuts	25 mL

Handful of fresh coriander leaves, finely chopped

Serves 4 or more.

Roasted Chilies

4 tbsp	vegetable oil	50 mL
4 oz	whole dry red chilies	125 g

Serves as a chili condiment for Thai as well as other dishes.

This lovely, smoky, fiery condiment is easy to make and lasts for 3-4 months if covered and refrigerated. But be warned: these are chilies and must be handled with care. Casual contact with sensitive areas (like eyes) can cause distress for endless minutes.

1. Heat oil in a wok (or frying pan) on high heat until it is just about to smoke. Lower heat to medium and add the chilies. Stir-fry for not more than 1 minute, until the chilies are shiny and have started to darken, but before they have turned black (if they have, they are burned, and you should discard them and start again).
2. Immediately transfer the chilies to a bowl to cool them down. Once cool, grind them (in a coffee grinder or processor) to coarse meal. Transfer to a jar and refrigerate, tightly covered.

SOUPS

⁓⋄⁓

A little note: lemon grass, galangal root and lime leaves, the trio of flavours that give many Thai soups their distinctive taste are unchewable, but form dictates that they be left in the soup. It is then up to the soup slurpers to avoid eating them. Furthermore, though lemon grass is easy to find, galangal root and lime leaves are not so easy. They can be substituted with ginger root and lime juice respectively as indicated in the recipes.

Tom Kha Kai
(Coconut-Chicken Soup)

4 oz	skinless, boneless chicken breast	125 g
1	stick lemon grass	1
1 inch	galangal root (OR ginger root)	2.5 cm
4	lime leaves (OR 1 tbsp/15 mL lime juice)	4
2	fresh hot chilies	2
2 cups	unsweetened coconut milk	500 mL
1 cup	water	250 mL
2 tbsp	lemon juice	25 mL
1 tbsp	fish sauce	15 mL
¼ tsp	sugar	1 mL

Fresh coriander leaves

Serves 4.

See note on lemon grass on page 41.

Aromatic and exotic, this soup manages to be soothing and familiar as well. It is probably its chicken content that makes it so comforting, but it is absolutely its spicing that has made it the most popular Thai soup on any menu. All that, plus total ease of execution: an absolute winner.

1. Slice chicken into thin (¼-inch/5-mm) strips. If you find it difficult to cut thinly through fresh meat, leave it in the freezer for 15-20 minutes to harden slightly and then slice. Reserve.
2. Smash lemon grass with the flat of a chef's knife once, and then cut it into 1-inch/2.5-cm pieces; slice galangal (or ginger) into thin rounds; tear lime leaves into thirds; cut chilies in half. Reserve all four of these mixed together in a bowl.
3. Heat coconut milk and water in a saucepan for 2-3 minutes. Don't let it boil. Reduce heat to medium and add reserved lemon grass/galangal/lime leaves/chilies and cook for another 2 minutes, stirring continuously and not letting it boil.
4. Add chicken strips and cook for 5 minutes, stirring over medium heat, until the chicken is cooked (don't overcook and lower heat if it threatens to boil).
5. Add lemon juice (plus lime juice if you haven't been able to find lime leaves), fish sauce and sugar. Stir, and continue cooking for another minute or two.
6. Transfer to a soup tureen and serve immediately, garnished with fresh coriander leaves.

Tom Yam Kai
(Lemon-Chicken Soup)

This is an alternate chicken soup to Tom Kha Kai *and although equally soothing, it has a livelier look and feel to it: it uses tomato to bolster its broth instead of coconut milk.*

8 oz	skinless, boneless chicken breast	250 g
1	stick lemon grass	1
1 inch	galangal root (OR ginger root)	2.5 cm
5	lime leaves (OR 2 tbsp/25 mL lime juice)	5
8 oz	fresh tomatoes	250 g
2 oz	button mushrooms	60 g
4 cups	water	1 L
4 tbsp	fish sauce	50 mL
1½ tsp	chili paste	7 mL
4 tbsp	lime juice	50 mL
2	fresh hot chilies	2

Fresh coriander leaves

Serves 4.

See note on lemon grass on page 41.

1. Slice the chicken into thin (¼-inch/5-mm) strips. If you find it difficult to cut thinly through fresh meat, leave it in the freezer for 15-20 minutes to harden slightly and then slice. Reserve.
2. Smash lemon grass with the flat of a chef's knife once, and then cut into 1-inch/2.5-cm pieces; slice galangal into thin rounds; tear lime leaves into thirds. Reserve these three ingredients together.
3. Wash and cut tomatoes into 1-inch/2.5-cm chunks. Reserve.
4. Cut mushrooms into halves (or quarters if large). Reserve.
5. Boil 4 cups/1 L water in a soup pot. Add reserved lemon grass/galangal/lime leaves and cook for 1 minute. Add fish sauce and cook for another minute. Add chili paste and reduce heat to medium. Add tomatoes and cook for 2-3 minutes, until the broth bubbles again. Add mushrooms and cook for one minute.
6. Turn heat to maximum and add the chicken strips. Stir to separate the strips and cook for 5 minutes until the chicken is done (but not overcooked).
7. Add 4 tbsp/50 mL lime juice (plus 2 tbsp/25 mL lime juice if you haven't used lime leaves). Stir.
8. Crush the fresh chilies and cut in half. Add the chilies to the soup and turn off heat. Transfer to a soup tureen, top with fresh coriander leaves and serve immediately.

Tom Yum Goong (Lemon Grass-Shrimp Soup)

4	cups water	1 L
1	stick lemon grass	1
4	lime leaves	4
	(OR 2 tbsp/25 mL lime juice)	
1 inch	galangal root	2.5 cm
	(OR ginger root)	
2	fresh hot chilies	2
3 tbsp	fish sauce	45 mL
1 tsp	sugar	5 mL
1½ tsp	chili paste	7 mL
2 oz	button mushrooms, quartered	60 g
16	large shrimps, shelled and deveined (10 oz/300 g)	16
3 tbsp	lime juice	45 mL

Fresh coriander leaves

Serves 4.

See note on lemon grass on page 41.

Quick and easy, this soup depends on its aromatics for its ethereal allure. The barely poached (definitely undercooked) shrimps, however, are what make it a treat.

1. Heat 4 cups/1 L water in a soup pot to boiling.
2. Smash the lemon grass with the flat of a chef's knife once, and then cut into 1-inch/2.5-cm pieces; tear the lime leaves into thirds; and slice the galangal into thin rounds. Reserve all three of these ingredients together.
3. Crush the fresh chilies and cut in half. Reserve separately.
4. When the water has boiled, add the reserved lemon grass/galangal/lime leaves. Boil for 1 minute. Add fish sauce, sugar and chili paste. Boil for another 2 minutes. Add mushrooms and boil for 2 minutes. Add shrimps and lime juice (3 tbsp/45 mL plus the other 2 tbsp/25 mL if you haven't used the lime leaves) and lower heat to medium-high. Cook for 2 minutes, just until the shrimps have turned white and springy. Transfer to a soup tureen, decorate with fresh coriander leaves and serve immediately.

Thai Hot and Sour Soup

This is a Thai version of our old favourite, the Chinese hot and sour soup. Hotter and more pleasant than its predecessor, Wandee offers it as a thick and lusty vegetarian specialty that truly satisfies.

1. Soak the black fungus in cold water for at least 30 minutes. When it has become shiny and slippery and swollen to 5-6 times its original size, wash it several times in running cold water and drain. Roughly chop and reserve.
2. Slice tofu in thin, long strips. Reserve.
3. Boil 4 cups/1 L water in a soup pot. Add soya sauce, black pepper, garlic, sugar, vinegar, chili-garlic sauce and salt. Lower heat to medium-high and cook for 2-3 minutes.
4. Add bamboo shoots and cook for 1 minute. Add reserved black fungus and cook another minute. Add reserved tofu and the sesame oil and cook for 3-5 minutes until everything seems to be settling. Meanwhile, dissolve the cornstarch with the water and stir into the soup, during the last 2 minutes of this cooking period.
5. Beat the egg yolks lightly and slide into the soup. Turn off the heat and DO NOT STIR. The egg will cook into the hot soup and stay in pieces (if stirred it'll disperse and become shrivelled). Transfer to a soup tureen and decorate with strips of red pepper and fresh coriander leaves. Serve immediately.

1 oz	dry black fungus	30 g
7 oz	fresh soft tofu	200 g
4 cups	water	1 L
3 tbsp	soya sauce	45 mL
½ tsp	black pepper	2 mL
1 tsp	chopped garlic	5 mL
1½ tsps	sugar	7 mL
5 tbsp	rice (or white) vinegar	70 mL
1 tsp	chili-garlic sauce	5 mL
¼ tsp	salt	1 mL
1 cup	bamboo shoot strips	250 mL
1 tsp	sesame oil	5 mL
1 tbsp	cornstarch	15 mL
1 tbsp	water	15 mL
2	egg yolks	2

Strips of red pepper
Fresh coriander leaves

Serves 4.

½ cup	cauliflower florets	125 mL
⅓ cup	broccoli florets	75 mL
⅓ cup	rough-chopped bok choy	75 mL
⅓ cup	rough-chopped white cabbage	75 mL
¼ cup	rough-chopped button mushrooms	50 mL
2 oz	snow peas	60 g
2 oz	baby corn (canned)	60 g
½ cup	tamarind paste	125 mL
½ cup	warm water	125 mL

Gang Som (Thai Country Soup)

A full-bodied soup, it is a meal-in-a-bowl if this recipe is served to two people instead of four, and accompanied by steamed rice. It's a big hit in the Thai countryside, where it never gets particularly cold, but during the long Canadian winter it promises to soothe exotically. It's easy to omit (or replace) a couple of its items to render it a vegetarian soup, as noted at the end of the recipe.

1. Deal with your vegetables: floret the cauliflower and broccoli, chop the bok choy, cabbage and mushrooms. Reserve all the ingredients together. Devein the snow peas and reserve together with the baby corn.
2. Soak the tamarind paste in warm water for 15 minutes. Mash it and transfer the mud-like mixture to a strainer set into a bowl. Mash and push with a spoon, forcing the liquid to strain into the bowl. Scrape off the juice that clings to the underside of the strainer. You'll have about 5 tbsp/70 mL of a thick, smooth, dark juice. Reserve. The solids left over in the strainer can be discarded.
3. Smash the lemon grass with the flat of a chef's knife once, and then slice into 1-inch/2.5-cm pieces; slice the galangal into thin rounds; tear the lime leaves into thirds. Reserve these ingredients together.
4. Boil 4 cups/1 L water in a soup pot. Add the reserved lemon grass/galangal/lime leaves and boil for 1 minute. Add fish sauce, chili paste and tamarind juice. Lower heat to medium and cook for 5 minutes.

5. Add reserved cauliflower, broccoli, bok choy, cabbage and mushrooms. Cook for 5 minutes, until the vegetables are heated through but still crunchy. Add reserved snow peas and baby corn. Cook for another 2 minutes.

6. Add shrimps and cook for 2 minutes, just until the shrimps have turned white and springy. Add 1 tbsp/15 mL lime juice (plus 1 tbsp/15 mL lime juice if you haven't used lime leaves), stir and turn off heat. Transfer to a soup tureen, top with fresh coriander leaves and serve immediately.

Variation:

Vegetarian Version: Replace fish sauce with ½ tsp/2 mL salt; replace chili paste with chili-garlic sauce; and omit shrimps altogether. Otherwise follow recipe exactly.

1	stick lemon grass	1
1 inch	galangal root	2.5 cm
	(OR fresh ginger root)	
2	lime leaves	2
	(OR 1 tbsp/15 mL lime juice)	
4 cups	water	1 L
3 tbsp	fish sauce	45 mL
1 tsp	chili paste	5 mL
8	large shrimps, shelled and deveined (5 oz/150 g)	8
1 tbsp	lime juice	15 mL

Fresh coriander leaves

Serves 4.

See note on lemon grass on page 41.

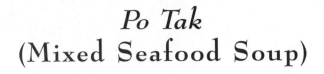

Po Tak
(Mixed Seafood Soup)

5 oz	trimmed kingfish	150 g
8	small crab claws	8
	(pre-cooked and frozen)	
8	large shrimps, shelled	8
	and deveined (5 oz/150 g)	
8	large mussels	8
	(preferably Kiwi)	
8 oz	cleaned squid	250 g
4 oz	button mushrooms	125 g
1	stick lemon grass	1
1 inch	galangal root	2.5 cm
	(OR ginger root)	
5	lime leaves	5
	(OR 2 tbsp/25 mL lime juice)	
5	cups water	1.25 L
5 tbsp	fish sauce	70 mL
3 tsp	chili paste	15 mL
5 tbsp	lime juice	70 mL
2	fresh hot chilies	2

Fresh coriander leaves

Serves 4 generously.

See note on lemon grass on page 41.

Whether it's called zarzuela *(in Spanish),* bouillabaise *(in French), or* kakavia *(in Greek), this flavourful soup, thick with seafood and fish, is bound to satisfy the fans of the treats from the deep. This one combines its maritime bounty with all the usual soup aromatics of Thai cuisine. Wonderful.*

1. Deal with the seafood: Cut kingfish into ½-inch/1-cm boneless cubes and reserve on its own. Wash crab claws; devein and wash shrimps; wash mussels; chop squid into ½-inch/ 1-cm pieces. Reserve these four ingredients together.
2. Quarter the mushrooms and reserve.
3. Smash the lemon grass with the flat of a chef's knife once, and then slice into 1-inch/2.5-cm pieces; slice the galangal into thin rounds; tear the lime leaves into thirds. Reserve these ingredients together.
4. Boil 5 cups/1.25 L water in a soup pot on medium-high heat. Add reserved lemon grass/galangal/lime leaves and cook for 2 minutes. Add fish sauce and chili paste and cook for another minute.
5. Add kingfish and cook for 2 minutes. Add rest of seafood and mushrooms and cook for 2 minutes, until the shrimps turn white and springy. Add 5 tbsp/70 mL lime juice (plus 2 tbsp/25 mL lime juice if you did not use lime leaves). Quickly crush the chilies with the flat of a chef's knife and add to the soup. Take off the fire and stir. Transfer to a soup tureen, top with fresh coriander leaves and serve.

SALADS

Yum Mamuang (Green Mango Salad) 50
    Vegetarian Version 51
Yum Woon Sen (Glass Noodle Salad) 52
Yum Goong (Steamed Shrimp Salad) 54
Som Tam (Green Papaya Salad) 55
Yum Talay (Seafood Salad) 56
Curry Salad 57
Yum Yai (Thai Royal Salad) 58
Yum Pla Muek (Spicy Squid Salad) 60

Yum Mamuang
(Green Mango Salad)

3 oz	skinless, boneless chicken breast	90 g
6	large shrimps, shelled and deveined 4 oz/125 g)	6
2 tbsp	vegetable oil	25 mL
1 tbsp	chopped garlic	15 mL
2	large green mangos	2
1 tbsp	fish sauce	15 mL
3 tbsp	sugar	45 mL
2 tbsp	chopped fresh coriander	25 mL
2 tbsp	chopped fresh mint	25mL
1/3	medium red pepper, in thin strips	1/3
1/2	small red onion, thinly sliced	1/2
2 tbsp	roasted unsalted peanuts	25 mL
3 tbsp	roasted unsalted cashews	45 mL

Fresh coriander leaves

Serves 4 or more.

Thai salad-making reaches its zenith with this sweet and sour concoction, whose main ingredient is a rather devilish type of mango that retains its tartness when ripe. There's only one way to shred a mango and though it appears to be a certain way to mutilate one's hand, Wandee assures me that it's perfectly safe and fast: in Thailand even children can do it. The final result is a lovely combination that is rich and satisfying, even though it contains precious little oil.

1. Place chicken breast and shelled shrimps on a board and, using a chef's knife, pound and chop until the two have been minced and thoroughly mixed. Heat 2 tbsp/25 mL vegetable oil in a frying pan and add garlic. Stir-fry for 30 seconds and add minced chicken-shrimp mixture. Stir-fry for 2-3 minutes on high heat, until the meats have separated into strands and appear cooked. Transfer to bowl to cool off. Reserve.

2. Peel the mangos (a vegetable peeler works well). Then take one mango in the palm of your hand and holding a sharp knife in the other, score deep gashes across the entire surface of the mango with clean, swift strokes (do this carefully). Then cut a thin layer off the top and watch the shreds fall into your work bowl. Continue on this side, until you have shredded down to the pit. Turn the mango around and repeat the process. Then do the other mango. By the end you should have quite a little hill of mango shreds. Good luck.

3. Add the reserved chicken-shrimp stir-fry to the mango shreds. Mix. Add fish sauce, sugar and chopped coriander and mint. Mix. Add red pepper strips and sliced onion. Mix. Process peanuts in a blender or processor till coarse meal. Add to salad and give the mixture a final toss and mix until it is well integrated.

4. Transfer to a serving bowl and scatter the cashews around the edges. Top with fresh coriander leaves. The salad is now ready and can be served immediately, or it can comfortably wait, unrefrigerated and lightly covered, for up to 1½ hours.

Variation:

Vegetarian Version: Omit the chicken, shrimp, vegetable oil, garlic and the fish sauce and step #1 of the procedure from the above recipe. Otherwise follow recipe, adding ¼ tsp/1 mL salt to compensate for the eliminated fish sauce.

Green mangoes are easily found in Asian markets. Don't be put off by the green skin; beneath it lurks a canary yellow, toothsome interior.

Yum Woon Sen
(Glass Noodle Salad)

4 oz	vermicelli bean threads	125 g
3 oz	skinless, boneless chicken breast	90 g
6	large shrimps, shelled and deveined (4 oz/125 g)	6
2 tbsp	vegetable oil	25 mL
1 tbsp	chopped garlic	15 mL
2	stems green onion, in ¼-inch/5-mm pieces	2
2 cups	water	500 mL
4	lime leaves (optional)	4
1	stick lemon grass	1
2 tbsp	chopped fresh coriander	25 mL
2 tbsp	chopped fresh mint	25 mL
⅓	medium red pepper, in thin strips	⅓
½	small red onion, thinly sliced	½
2 tbsp	roasted unsalted peanuts	25 mL
5 tbsp	lime juice	70 mL
3 tbsp	fish sauce	45 mL
1 tbsp	sugar	15 mL
2	fresh hot chilies, finely chopped	2

Similar in aromatics and ingredients to the mango salad, this one uses transparent bean threads (or glass noodles) as the base ingredient and as such it is more substantial. It works well as a companion piece to the mango salad and the two can be conveniently concocted simultaneously, simply by doubling up the ingredients.

1. Immerse vermicelli bean threads in a pot of cold water to soak for about 1 hour.
2. Place chicken breast and shelled shrimps on a board and, using a chef's knife, pound and chop until the two have been minced and thoroughly mixed. Heat 2 tbsp/25 mL vegetable oil in a frying pan and add garlic. Stir-fry for 30 seconds and add minced chicken-shrimp mixture. Stir-fry for 2-3 minutes on high heat, until the meats have separated into strands and appear cooked. Transfer to a work bowl and reserve. Add the green onion pieces and mix lightly.
3. Heat 2 cups/500 mL water in a soup pot. Add 4 lime leaves, torn into thirds, and one stick lemon grass, smashed with the flat of a chef's knife once, and then chopped into 1-inch/2.5-cm pieces. Let it come to a boil and boil for 1 minute.
4. Drain noodles from their (step #1) soaking water and add them to the boiling water. Cook for 30 seconds. The noodles will instantly turn translucent. Drain immediately into a strainer. Pick out lemon grass and lime leaf pieces and discard. Add the noodles to the bowl with the meats. Toss gently a couple of times.

5. Add chopped coriander and mint, red pepper strips, red onion slices, and peanuts. Toss lightly after each addition.
6. In a small bowl combine lime juice, fish sauce, sugar and chopped chilies. Mix well to dissolve sugar and then sprinkle this dressing evenly over the noodle salad. Toss to distribute dressing and ingredients but without unduly breaking the noodles.
7. Transfer to a serving platter and top with fresh coriander leaves. This salad is now ready and can be served immediately, slightly warm. It can also wait for up to 1½ hours, unrefrigerated and lightly covered. Accompany with Young Thailand Hot Sauce *(page 37)* if you like things very hot.

Fresh coriander leaves
Young Thailand Hot Sauce
(optional)

Serves 4 or more.

See note on lemon grass on page 41.

Thai salads are served in no particular order during a meal. All appetizers, even soups, can be served anytime: Thai meals are meant to be celebrations of the variety and colourful profusion of the national cuisine.

Yum Goong
(Steamed Shrimp Salad)

Here is yet another excuse to enjoy shrimps, which the Thai like almost as much as we do. This is a hot and zippy shrimp cocktail at heart, but a far cry from the old ring of overcooked creatures stuck round the rim of an ice-cream glass with the stodgy red sauce in the middle.

24	large shrimps, shelled and deveined (15 oz/450 g)	24
1½	cups water	375 mL
4	lime leaves (optional)	4
1	stick lemon grass	1
½	lemon, juice and rind	1/2
1 tbsp	fish sauce	15 mL
3 tbsp	lime juice	45 mL
3 tsp	chili paste	15 mL
½	medium red pepper, in thin strips	½
½	medium red onion, thinly sliced	½
2 tbsp	roughly chopped mint	25 mL
2 tbsp	roughly chopped basil	25 mL
2 tbsp	roughly chopped fresh coriander	25 mL

Lettuce leaves
Fresh coriander leaves
Slices of orange
Wedges of lemon or lime

Serves 4.

1. Wash and reserve shrimps.
2. Heat 1½ cups/375 mL water in a saucepan. Add the lime leaves torn into thirds and the lemon grass, smashed with the flat of a chef's knife once, and then chopped in 1-inch/2.5-cm pieces. Squeeze lemon into the water and also add the rind. Let it come to a boil and cook for 1 minute.
3. Add the shrimps and cook for not much more than a minute, stirring until the shrimps have turned white and springy. Drain immediately and transfer to a work bowl. Discard all the aromatics (lemon rind, lemon grass, lime leaves) and allow the shrimps to cool off for 1 or 2 minutes.
4. Add fish sauce, lime juice and chili paste to shrimps. Toss and turn to mix well and thoroughly coat the shrimps. Add red pepper strips, sliced red onion, and all the roughly chopped herbs (mint, basil, coriander). Toss and mix well.
5. Transfer to a serving plate that is lined with lettuce leaves. Decorate with fresh coriander leaves, slices of orange and wedges of lemon or lime. The salad can be served immediately or it can wait up to 1 hour, unrefrigerated and lightly covered.

Som Tam
(Green Papaya Salad)

This delightful cousin of the green mango salad uses totally unripe (read: rock hard) green papaya, which happily for us, lends itself to being grated (though a Thai chef would still prefer to hand-hold the papaya and stroke it with a sharp knife in the manner of the green mango). In assembling this salad a large-size mortar and pestle are essential; otherwise it's not authentic.

1. Peel the papaya, cut into quarters and scoop out and discard the pips. Grate through the largest holes of the grater to obtain about 1½ - 2 cups/375-500 mL of papaya shreds.
2. Put garlic into a large mortar. Chop chili into quarters and add to garlic. Wash and drain dried shrimps and add to mortar. Add peanuts. Pound these ingredients with the pestle until they begin to break up.
3. Trim the ends and cut long beans into 1-inch/2.5-cm pieces. Add to mortar and pound for 1 minute. Add papaya shreds and pound. Cut tomato into eighths and add to mortar. Pound for another minute.
4. Add sugar, fish sauce and lime juice and pound, working the material from the bottom to the top. The salad is ready when everything has been integrated, some juice has been extracted and all the bigger chunks have been broken down. The ingredients should not be crushed to a pulp, especially not the papaya. (A processor would be totally inappropriate, as it would turn everything to mush.)
5. Transfer to serving dish and top with fresh coriander leaves. The salad can be served immediately, or it can wait up to 1½ hours, unrefrigerated and lightly covered.

1	small green papaya	1
1 tsp	chopped garlic	5 mL
1	fresh hot chili	1
2 tbsp	Thai dried shrimps	25 mL
1 tbsp	roasted unsalted peanuts	15 mL
3	long green beans	3
1	medium tomato	1
3 tsp	sugar	15 mL
2 tbsp	fish sauce	25 mL
3 tbsp	lime juice	45 mL

Fresh coriander leaves

Serves 4.

This recipe provides a good excuse to buy a mortar and pestle, which is much preferable to the food processor for many procedures, and certainly looks decorative in any kitchen.

Yum Talay
(Seafood Salad)

1	stick lemon grass	1
5 oz	cleaned squid	150 g
8	large shrimps, shelled and deveined (5 oz/150 g)	8
8	large mussels (preferably Kiwi)	8
8	small crab claws (pre-cooked and frozen)	8
1	fresh hot chili, cut into thirds	1
1 tsp	chopped garlic	5 mL
4 tbsp	lime juice	50 mL
2 tbsp	fish sauce	25 mL
1 tsp	sugar	5 mL
2 tbsp	chili paste	25 mL
1/3	medium red pepper, in thin strips	1/3
1/2	small red onion, thinly sliced	1/2
2 tbsp	fresh basil	25 mL
2 tbsp	fresh mint	25 mL
2 tbsp	fresh coriander	25 mL

Fresh coriander leaves
Wedges of lime
Young Thailand Hot Sauce

Serves 4.

Tart and herb-flavoured seafood that has been lightly poached is a refreshing favourite of all nations with a seaside culture, and Thailand is no exception. This is a luxurious salad that is very easy to create and especially fun to eat in summer, outdoors, with a view (if possible) of a large body of water.

1. Boil 3 cups/750 mL water in a saucepan. Smash lemon grass with the flat of chef's knife once and chop into 1-inch/2.5-cm pieces. Add to water and boil for 2 minutes.
2. Slice squid into 1/2-inch/1-cm rings. Add the squid as well as the rest of the seafood to the boiling water and cook for 2 minutes on high heat, until the shrimps are white and springy. Immediately transfer to a strainer and drain all the water. Reserve in strainer.
3. In a small bowl combine hot chili pieces, garlic, lime juice, fish sauce, sugar and chili paste. Beat to mix thoroughly. Reserve.
4. Toss seafood in its strainer to remove all additional liquid. Transfer seafood, including the lemon grass pieces, to a work bowl. Add the reserved dressing (from step #3) and toss to coat everything thoroughly. Add red pepper strips, red onion slices and chopped herbs (basil, mint, coriander) and toss again to integrate.
5. Transfer to a serving dish, top with fresh coriander leaves and lime wedges along the sides. This salad can be served immediately, or it can wait up to 1 1/2 hours, unrefrigerated and lightly covered. Serve Young Thailand Hot Sauce (*page 37*) on the side.

THE YOUNG THAILAND COOKBOOK

Curry Salad

A composite salad of all our favourite ingredients, it makes a wonderful warm-weather light lunch or a substantial starter course for a festive dinner. It depends for its attraction on the peanut dressing and provides a good use for leftover Peanut Sauce which has been in the freezer since the last dinner party's satay starters. The tofu, which is best if fried fresh, can in fact be bought already fried, or if eschewing the extra calories, can be used raw.

½ cup	vegetable oil	125 mL
4 oz	fresh pressed tofu	125 g
4	lettuce leaves	4
	(preferably curly)	
1 cup	bean sprouts	250 mL
⅓ cup	grated carrot	75 mL
½	small onion, thinly sliced	½
2	medium tomatoes,	2
	in thin wedges	
2 inches	English	5 cm
	cucumber, sliced	
½	medium red pepper,	½
	in thin strips	
4	boiled eggs, shelled	4
	and quartered	
1 cup	Peanut Sauce	250 mL
4 tbsp	unsweetened coconut	50 mL
	milk (OR water)	

Additional strips of red pepper
and grated carrot
Fresh coriander leaves

Serves 4.

1. Heat ½ cup/125 mL vegetable oil in a small frying pan to almost smoking and add tofu. Fry first side on high heat for 3 minutes, turn, lower heat to medium-high and fry second side for 3-5 minutes until golden. Remove from the oil and drain excess fat on a paper towel, lay on a board and cut into thin squares. Reserve.

2. Assemble this salad on 4 separate plates using a quarter of the ingredients for each. Tear one lettuce leaf in chunks and lay on the plate. Add bean sprouts, tofu, carrot, onion, tomatoes, cucumber, red pepper and egg decoratively, avoiding over layering as much as possible. The salads can wait at this stage, covered tightly but not refrigerated.

3. Heat Peanut Sauce, if from frozen, and add coconut milk, stirring to thin it out. Do not allow to boil. Let it cool down somewhat. (If using freshly made Peanut Sauce *(page 36)*, dilute 1 cup/250 mL of it with warm coconut milk and again, let it cool down somewhat). Nap the salads with the sauce, using about a quarter of it per salad.

4. Top the salads with some additional red pepper strips, grated carrot and fresh coriander leaves. Serve immediately.

Yum Yai
(Thai Royal Salad)

4 oz	Thai sausage (OR other ham)	125 g
8	large shrimps, shelled and deveined (5 oz/150 g)	8
4 oz	skinless, boneless chicken breast	125 g
1/2 tsp	salt	2 mL
1 1/2 tsp	sugar	7 mL
1 tsp	chopped garlic	5 mL
2 tbsp	fish sauce	25 mL
3 tbsp	lime juice	45 mL
2	fresh hot chilies, finely chopped	2
4	lettuce leaves (preferably curly)	4
1/3	medium red pepper, in thin strips	1/3
1/2	small red onion, thinly sliced	1/2
1/3 cup	grated carrot	75 mL
2 inches	English cucumber,	5 cm
1	medium tomato, thinly sliced	1

The salad is a hefty affair, like our chef's salad (only in this case, "a king's salad"), which combines a number of favourite ingredients in a sauce that echoes all the other Thai salads. The novelty here is the use of Thai sausage, which is available in Asian stores. Wandee grudgingly agrees that ordinary ham can be substituted, if that will make it easier to contemplate this recipe, which makes a fun lunch on its own and also works well as the main salad in a buffet of appetizers.

1. Slice Thai sausage (or ham) thinly in 1-inch x 3-inch/2.5-cm x 7.5-cm strips. Reserve along with the shelled, deveined shrimps. Slice chicken into 1/4-inch/5-mm strips. If you find it difficult to cut thinly through fresh meat, leave it in the freezer for 15-20 minutes to harden slightly and then slice. Reserve on its own.
2. Boil 2-3 cups/500-750 mL water with salt in a saucepan. Add chicken and cook, stirring, for 1 1/2 minutes. Add sausage and shrimps and cook for 1-1 1/2 minutes, stirring until the shrimps have turned white and springy (do not overcook). Immediately transfer into a strainer to drain. Reserve in strainer.
3. In a small bowl combine sugar, garlic, fish sauce, lime juice and chopped chilies. Beat to mix thoroughly. Reserve.
4. Break lettuce leaves in chunks into a salad bowl. Toss meats in the strainer to remove all additional liquid. Add to the lettuce. Sprinkle half the dressing (from step #3) over the salad and toss to coat and combine.

5. Add red pepper, red onion, carrot, cucumber and tomato. Add the rest of the reserved dressing and toss to mix and coat everything thoroughly. Sprinkle with the chopped herbs (mint and coriander) and top with the cashews. Serve within 15 minutes, before the lettuce begins to wilt unduly.

2 tbsp	roughly chopped fresh mint	25 mL
2 tbsp	roughly chopped fresh coriander	25 mL
¼ cup	roasted unsalted cashews	50 mL

Serves 4.

Legend has it that some 200 years ago, King Rama II's much beloved wife invented this salad for him, and he countered with a song in its (and her) honour. Both song and salad have survived.

The song, which is taught at schools as an obligatory rhyme, says:

*"Yum Yai, the salad of many vegetables
Arrange them with beauty
Yum Yai tasty with nam pla
Everyone'll crave it"*

Yum Pla Muek
(Spicy Squid Salad)

10 oz	cleaned squid	300 g
1	stick lemon grass	1
1 tsp	sugar	5 mL
1 tbsp	chopped garlic	15 mL
2 tbsp	fish sauce	25 mL
3 tbsp	lime juice	45 mL
1 tsp	chili-garlic sauce	5 mL
1 tsp	chili paste	5 mL
2 tbsp	roughly chopped fresh mint	25 mL
2 tbsp	roughly chopped fresh coriander	25 mL
½	small red onion, thinly sliced	½
⅓	medium red pepper, in thin strips	⅓
1	stem green onion	1

Additional strips of red pepper
Fresh coriander leaves

Serves 4.

A palate awakener, it transforms the lowly squid into a delicacy without assaulting the pocketbook. When cooked as delicately as in this recipe, squid offers one of those dream textures that only undercooked seafood can: crisp and soft simultaneously. The multi-flavoured dressing adds the necessary zip and the ease of execution is just simply a bonus.

1. Slice squid into ½-inch/1-cm rings. Reserve.
2. Smash lemon grass with the flat of a chef's knife once and chop into 1-inch/2.5-cm pieces.
3. Boil 2-3 cups/500-750 mL water in a saucepan. Add lemon grass and let boil for 1 minute. Add squid and cook for 1 minute (do not overcook). Immediately transfer into a strainer to drain. Discard lemon grass pieces. Reserve squid in strainer.
4. In a small bowl combine sugar, garlic, fish sauce, lime juice, chili-garlic and chili paste. Beat to mix thoroughly. Reserve.
5. Toss squid in its strainer to remove all additional liquid. Transfer to a work bowl. Add reserved dressing (from step #4) and toss to coat thoroughly. Add herbs (mint and coriander), red onion and red pepper. Chop green onion in ¼-inch/5-mm pieces, and add to the bowl. Toss to integrate all the ingredients of the salad.
6. Transfer to a serving dish and top with additional red pepper strips and fresh coriander leaves. This salad is now ready and can be served immediately, or it can wait up to 1½ hours, unrefrigerated and lightly covered.

NOODLES

Rice Noodle Salad   62

Pad Thai (Thai Noodles)   64

Phad Woon Sen (Glass Noodles with Chicken)   66

Mee Ka-Thi (Coconut Noodles with Chicken and Shrimps)   68

Thai Spicy Noodles   70

Radnar Talay (Thai Noodles With Seafood)   71

Rice Noodle Salad

8 oz	Thai rice noodles	250 g
1¼ cups	bean sprouts	150 mL
8 oz	skinless, boneless chicken breast	250 g
5 tbsp	vegetable oil	70 mL
1 tsp	chopped garlic	5 mL
1 tbsp	soya sauce	15 mL
2 tbsp	roughly chopped fresh coriander	25 mL
1	stem green onion	1
2 tbsp	sugar	25 mL
3 tbsp	fish sauce	45 mL
4 tbsp	lime juice	50 mL
½ tsp	roasted chilies	2 mL
¼ cup	roasted unsalted peanuts	50 mL

Some additional peanuts
Strips of red pepper
Wedges of lime
Fresh coriander leaves
YOUNG THAILAND Hot Sauce

Serves 4.

Pasta salad, which these days threatens to take over from cole slaw and potato salad in lunch-time prominence, will never again be the same when this simple rice noodle salad hits the headlines. Based on the miraculous "rice stick", the Thai answer to pasta heaven, it requires precious little cooking and is, therefore, basically mistake-proof.

1. Soak noodles in plenty of cold water for at least 1 hour. Then boil 3-4 cups/750 mL-1 L of water in a wok (or deep frying pan). Drain noodles from their soaking water and add to boiling water. Boil stirring for a mere 30 seconds. They will have reduced to half of their original volume. Drain immediately, and transfer to a work bowl.

2. Heat 2 cups/500 mL water in the same wok and add bean sprouts. Cook at high heat for 30 seconds and drain. They will become darker but should still be crunchy. Drain immediately and add to noodles.

3. Slice the chicken into ¼-inch/5-mm strips. If you find it difficult to cut thinly through fresh meat, leave it in the freezer for 15-20 minutes to harden slightly and then slice. Heat 5 tbsp/70 mL oil in a wok (or frying pan) until it is just about to smoke. Add garlic and stir; immediately add chicken and stir-fry for 1 minute. Add soya sauce and stir-fry at medium-high heat for about 3 more minutes until the chicken is cooked, but not overcooked. Take off fire and add to the noodles in the bowl, and lightly toss to begin the mixing procedure. Add chopped coriander. Chop the green onion into ¼-inch/5-mm pieces and add to the salad and toss once again.

4. In a small bowl combine sugar, fish sauce, lime juice and roasted chilies *(page 40)*. Beat to mix thoroughly. Sprinkle evenly over the salad and toss again to mix.

5. Process peanuts in a blender or processor to coarse meal. Sprinkle over the salad and toss several times to integrate all the ingredients (toss gently, so as not to unduly break the noodles).

6. Transfer to a serving dish and top with whole peanuts, red pepper strips, lime wedges and fresh coriander leaves. This salad is now ready. It can wait for up to 1½ hours, unrefrigerated and lightly covered. Serve with a side bowl of YOUNG THAILAND Hot Sauce *(page 37)*.

This salad is one of the few Thai offerings that lends itself to accompaniment by recipes from other cuisines: a perfect touch of exotica for a party buffet.

Pad Thai
(Thai Noodles)

8 oz	Thai rice noodles	250 g
¼ cup	tamarind paste	50 mL
¼ cup	warm water	50 mL
4 oz	skinless, boneless chicken breast	125 g
4 oz	fried tofu	125 g
6 tbsp	roasted unsalted peanuts	75 mL
3 tbsp	fish sauce	45 mL
2 tbsp	sugar	25 mL
2 tbsp	lime juice	25 mL
½ cup	vegetable oil	125 mL
1 tsp	chopped garlic	
8	large shrimps, shelled and deveined (50 oz/150 g)	8
2	eggs	2
1 cup	bean sprouts	250 mL
2	stems green onion, in 1-inch/2.5-cm pieces	2

This is the one noodle dish to master, and to love, over all the others (including the best that Italy has to offer). It's so addictive that it alone would keep Thai cuisine alive in Canada, were we ever to become too jaded for our own good and eschewed everything else.

Pad Thai is a splendid lesson in how the simple, and bland, rice stick (a.k.a. rice vermicelli) can evolve in the culinary hands of a tasteful culture. The result is so harmonious, so perfect in every way, that it would be hard to imagine it without even one of its vast symphony of flavours and ingredients. Though daunting at first (so many ingredients), it is actually relatively easy to concoct. The only caveat is that one cannot stint on the oil content, although it appears excessive. Too little oil, the noodles will stick and you'll have a mess in your wok. I've gotten away with 5 tbsp/70 mL instead of the full ½ cup/125 mL but I had to work awfully fast to avoid the sticking. This one is a treat; give it its full due and it'll pay back in memorable pleasure.

1. Soak noodles in plenty of cold water for at least 1 hour.
2. Combine tamarind paste with a ¼ cup/50 mL warm water in a small bowl and let soak for at least 15 minutes.
3. Slice the chicken into ¼-inch/5-mm strips. If you find it difficult to cut thinly through fresh meat, leave it in the freezer for 15-20 minutes to harden slightly and then slice. Reserve.
4. Slice the fried tofu into ¾-inch/1.5-cm cubes. Reserve.
5. Blend or process peanuts into coarse meal. Reserve.
6. Return to your reserved tamarind paste in its water. Mash it and transfer the mud-like mixture to a strainer set into a bowl. Mash and push with a spoon, forcing liquid to strain

into the bowl. Scrape off the juice that clings to the underside of the strainer. You will have about 5 tbsp/70 mL of tamarind juice. Add to it the fish sauce, sugar and lime juice. Beat to thoroughly mix and reserve. Discard the solids left in the strainer.

½ tsp	roasted chilies	2 mL

Strips of red pepper
Fresh coriander leaves
Wedges of lime

*Serves 4 as a noodle course or
2 as a main course.*

7. Heat oil in a wok (or large frying pan) until it is just about to smoke. Add garlic and stir, letting it cook for about 30 seconds. Add chicken and stir-fry for 1 minute. Add tofu and shrimps and stir-fry for 1 more minute. Break eggs into wok and let them fry without breaking them up for 1-2 minutes.

8. While eggs cook, quickly drain the noodles and then add to wok, giving them a quick fold, stir-frying for 1 minute from the bottom up. Add reserved tamarind juice, etc. (from step #6) and continue stir-frying, mixing everything together for 1-2 minutes. Your noodles will have subsided to half their original volume and softened up to al dente.

9. Add about ⅔ of the reserved ground peanuts and stir. Add about ⅔ of the bean sprouts and all the green onion pieces. Stir-fry for 30 seconds and take off heat.

10. Transfer noodles to a serving dish and sprinkle roasted chilies *(page 40)*. Top with the rest of the ground peanuts, the rest of the sprouts, some strips of red pepper and fresh coriander leaves. Stick a couple of lime wedges on the side and serve immediately.

Phad Woon Sen (Glass Noodles with Chicken)

4 oz	glass noodles (bean threads)	125 g
3 tbsp	black fungus	45 mL
6 oz	skinless, boneless chicken breast	175 g
7 tbsp	vegetable oil	95 mL
1 tsp	chopped garlic	5 mL
2	eggs	2
2 tbsp	soya sauce	25 mL
½ tsp	black pepper	2 mL
1 tsp	sugar	5 mL
1 tbsp	oyster sauce	15 mL
6 tbsp	water	75 mL
1 tsp	dark soya sauce	5 mL
1 tsp	sesame oil	5 mL
½	small onion, roughly chopped	½
1	stem green onion, in 1-inch/2.5-cm pieces	1

Eating glass noodles is like participating in culinary magic. For me, ordinary noodles are in themselves the result of some fairly astounding innovation, but consider glass noodles: derived from the flour of a bean (the mung), they are ultra-thin, and they turn transparent after cooking, while maintaining a soothing slurpability. Not only magic, but pure pleasure; especially when dressed up with the lovely treats of this recipe.

1. Soak glass noodles in plenty of cold water for about 1 hour. Separately soak black fungus in plenty of cold water, also for 1 hour. At the end of the soaking period, transfer the noodles to a strainer, drain out all the excess water (the noodles will have swollen to about 3 times their original volume) and reserve in the strainer. Now turning to the black fungus (it'll have swollen to 5-6 times its original size and become shiny and slightly slippery), wash it several times in cold running water, drain and reserve.

2. Slice the chicken in strips that are ¼ inch/5 mm thick, 2 inches/5 cm long and about 1 inch/2.5 cm wide. If you find it difficult to cut thinly through fresh meat, leave it in the freezer for 15-20 minutes to harden slightly, and then slice. Reserve.

3. Heat oil in a wok (or frying pan) on high heat until it is just about to smoke. Add garlic and stir-fry for 30 seconds. Add chicken and stir-fry for 1 minute. Turn heat down to medium

Pinch black pepper
Strips of red pepper
Fresh coriander leaves
YOUNG THAILAND Hot Sauce

and stir-fry for 1-2 minutes more, until the chicken has warmed through and turned white. Break the eggs directly into the wok. Increase heat to medium-high and fry the eggs without breaking them up for 2 minutes, until they're partially set.

4. Push the eggs and chicken to one side of the wok, and add the reserved, drained noodles and black fungus to the other side. Take wok off the fire, and add the soya sauce, black pepper, sugar, oyster sauce, water and dark soya sauce to the noodles, sprinkling evenly. Return wok to the fire and using a shovelling motion, combine the contents of the two sides, tossing-stirring for 2 minutes, working from the bottom up, so that all the noodles have a chance to fry in the oil, and everything is integrated.

5. Add sesame oil, onion and green onion and toss stir for 1 minute. Take off fire and transfer to a serving dish. Sprinkle with black pepper, and top with red pepper strips and fresh coriander leaves. Serve immediately with YOUNG THAILAND Hot Sauce (*page 37*) on the side.

*Serves 2 as a main course or
4 as a noodle course.*

Mee Ka-Thi
(Coconut Noodles with Chicken and Shrimps)

8 oz	thin rice sticks (rice vermicelli)	250 g
2 tbsp	tamarind paste	25 mL
2 tbsp	warm water	25 mL
4 oz	skinless, boneless chicken breast	125 g
8	large shrimps, shelled and deveined (5 oz/150 g)	8
1 tbsp	vegetable oil	15 mL
1 tsp	chopped garlic	5 mL
½	medium onion, roughly chopped	½
2 cups	unsweetened coconut milk	500 mL
1 tbsp	salted soya beans	15 mL
1 tbsp	sugar	15 mL
1 tsp	fish sauce	5 mL
1 tsp	tomato paste	5 mL
1 tbsp	water	15 mL
1 tbsp	fish sauce	15 mL
1 cup	bean sprouts	250 mL
2	stems green onion, in 1-inch/2.5-cm pieces	2
1 tbsp	vegetable oil	15 mL
2	eggs	2

This is a complex recipe with three consecutive procedures that must be carried out speedily, resulting in a three-tiered noodle dish that satisfies the palate while exciting the senses. It is relatively grease-free; rich and redolent with coconut milk and tamarind sauce and salted soya beans—all those exotic ingredients that transport us to a place of palm trees swaying to sweet sea breezes.

1. The rice sticks of this recipe are much thinner than the ones in the previous recipes. They must be soaked in plenty of cold water like their thicker counterparts but for only 15 minutes. Any longer would over-soften them.
2. Combine tamarind paste with the warm water and let soak for 15 minutes. Then mash it and transfer the mud-like mixture to a strainer set into a bowl. Mash and push with a spoon, forcing liquid to strain into the bowl. Scrape off juice that clings to the underside of the strainer. You'll have about 2 tbsp/25 mL of tamarind juice. Reserve it. The solids left over in the strainer can be discarded.
3. Turn back to your noodles which have been soaking for the last 15 minutes. Strain them and reserve in the strainer.
4. Now, turning to your chicken and shrimp, place them together on a board and, using a chef's knife, pound and chop until minced and thoroughly combined. Reserve.
5. Heat 1 tbsp/15 mL oil in a wok (or frying pan) until it is just about to smoke. Add garlic and stir-fry for 30 seconds. Add onion and stir-fry for 1 minute. Add 1 cup/250 mL of the

coconut milk and stir-fry for 1-2 minutes, until bubbling hard. Add the shrimp-chicken mince and stir-cook for 2 minutes until the meats break up and appear to be cooked. Quickly add the salted soya beans, sugar, reserved tamarind juice and 1 tsp/5 mL of the fish sauce, stirring after each addition. Cook for 2 minutes more, stirring until it's all bubbling and thickening. Transfer to a bowl and cover.

6. In another wok (or frying pan) heat the remaining 1 cup/ 250 mL of the coconut milk. Combine tomato paste with water and add along with 3 tsp/15 mL of the fish sauce until the liquids are bubbling. Add strained noodles to the wok, stirring for 2 minutes with a shovelling motion, to moisten all the noodles in the coconut milk. Add ¾ of the bean sprouts and all the green onion, stirring into the noodles for 1 minute. Transfer to a serving dish and immediately top with the reserved shrimp-chicken stir-fry. Cover to keep warm, while you proceed with one final step.

7. Heat 1 tbsp/15 mL oil in a frying pan. Beat the eggs lightly in a bowl. Add to the oil and fry them for 2-3 minutes, pulling them in from the sides, in a manner that would be a cross between omelette and scrambled. Do not overcook. Take off the fire and break them up into large chunks. Top the noodle dish with this egg and decorate with red pepper strips and fresh coriander leaves. Garnish the sides with slices of cucumber. Serve immediately with a side bowl of YOUNG THAILAND Hot Sauce *(page 37)*.

Strips of red pepper
Fresh coriander leaves
Slices of cucumber
YOUNG THAILAND Hot Sauce

Serves 2-4.

Thai Spicy Noodle

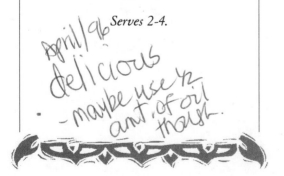

8 oz	Thai rice noodles	250 g
8 oz	trimmed pork tenderloin	250 g
½	medium red pepper	½
½	medium green pepper	½
5 tbsp	vegetable oil	70 mL
1 tsp	chopped garlic	5 mL
4	fresh hot chilies, finely chopped	4
2 tbsp	soya sauce	25 mL
1 tsp	sugar	5 mL
1 tbsp	oyster sauce	15 mL
3 tbsp	water	45 mL
20	whole leaves fresh basil	20
½ tsp	cornstarch	2 mL
1 tbsp	water	15 mL

Young Thailand Hot Sauce

Serves 2-4.

April/96 delicious — maybe use ½ amt. of oil than.

A bed of steamed noodles is topped with a saucy, spicy stir-fry of meat and vegetables, aromatically enhanced with basil leaves. This hearty dish will satisfy serious appetites, but also tempt more delicate constitutions. It can be a full meal for two, or the noodle course of a dinner for four. The pork can be substituted with chicken or beef.

1. Soak noodles in plenty of cold water for at least 1 hour.
2. Slice pork into ¼-inch/5-mm strips and reserve. If you find it difficult to cut thinly through fresh meat, leave it in the freezer for 15-20 minutes to harden slightly and then slice.
3. Cut red and green peppers into 1-inch/2.5-cm squares. Reserve.
4. Heat oil in a wok (or frying pan) until it is just about to smoke. Add garlic and chilies and stir-fry for 30 seconds. Add pork strips and stir-fry for 2 minutes. Add soya sauce, sugar, oyster sauce and water and stir-fry another 2 minutes. Add red and green pepper squares and ¾ of the basil leaves, stir and let cook for 2-3 minutes until the peppers have just begun to soften.
5. Take wok off the fire and do two quick chores. First, put 3 cups/750 mL of water to boil in a soup pot. Second, dissolve ½ tsp/2 mL cornstarch in 1 tbsp/15 mL cold water in a small bowl and add to the wok and stir. Return to the fire and stir-cook for 1 minute (the sauce around the meat will thicken somewhat). Take off fire and cover.
4. Drain noodles and add to boiling water in the soup pot. Cook, stirring for 30 seconds. Drain and transfer to a serving dish. Transfer the reserved pork stir-fry with its sauce to top of noodles. Decorate with remaining basil leaves and serve immediately with a side bowl of Young Thailand Hot Sauce *(page 37).*

Radnar Talay
(Thai Noodles With Seafood)

Similar in concept to the previous recipe, this one presents the same bed of noodles topped with a juicy stir-fry of feathery seafood. Again, this recipe will serve either as a meal for two hearty appetites or as the middle course of a dinner for four. Wandee offers this dish without chilies, but it can be perked up with hot sauce if you want. Otherwise, it can be spiked with the chili-less Lemon-Coriander Sauce.

1. Soak noodles in plenty of cold water for at least 1 hour.
2. Slice squid into 1-inch/2.5-cm rings and reserve along with the shelled, deveined shrimps.
3. Chop Asian greens into 1-inch/2.5-cm pieces. Pick out the florets from the broccoli: you should have 15-20 pieces (save stalk for future use, such as stock-making). Remove strings of the snow peas. Reserve all three vegetables together.
4. Heat oil in a wok or frying pan until it is just about to smoke. Add garlic and stir-fry for 30 seconds. Add reserved seafood and stir-fry for 30 seconds. Add reserved vegetables and stir-fry for 1 minute until they start to wilt. Add fish sauce, oyster sauce, sugar, soya sauce, 1 cup/250 mL water and black pepper. Stir, and let cook on medium heat for 3-4 minutes.
5. Now find time for two quick operations: put 3 cups/750 mL water to boil in a soup pot; dissolve cornstarch in 1 tbsp/ 15 mL cold water.

8 oz	Thai rice noodles	250 g
4 oz	cleaned squid	125 g
8	large shrimps, shelled	8
	and deveined (5 oz/150 g)	
3	leaves Asian greens	3
	(e.g. bok choy)	
1	branch broccoli	1
2 oz	snow peas	60 g
5 tbsp	vegetable oil	70 mL
1 tsp	chopped garlic	5 mL
1 tbsp	fish sauce	15 mL
2 tbsp	oyster sauce	25 mL
1 tsp	sugar	5 mL
1 tbsp	soya sauce	15 mL
1 cup	water	250 mL
1/2 tsp	black pepper	2 mL
1 tsp	cornstarch	5 mL
1 tbsp	water	15 mL

Fresh coriander leaves
Strips of red pepper
Thai Lemon-Coriander Sauce or
YOUNG THAILAND Hot Sauce

Serves 2-4.

A final word about these amazing Thai rice noodles that are so easy and fast to prepare. Quick boiled, as in this recipe, they serve as a perfect bed for any stir-fry in your repertoire, and make a welcome alternative to steamed rice.

6. Returning to your wok with the seafood stir-fry, add the dissolved cornstarch, stir, lower heat to medium-low and cook for 1-2 minutes until the sauce thickens somewhat. Take off fire and reserve the stir-fry in the wok uncovered. (Covering it would continue to cook the seafood and toughen it.)

7. Drain the soaking noodles and add to the boiling water in the soup pot. Cook stirring for 30 seconds. Drain and transfer to a serving dish. Place the reserved seafood-vegetable stir-fry with all its sauce on top of the noodles. Decorate with fresh coriander leaves and red pepper strips. Serve immediately with either Thai Lemon-Coriander *(page 39)* or YOUNG THAILAND Hot Sauce *(page 37)*, or both.

RICE

Khao Phad Kai (Thai Chicken Fried Rice)   74

Vegetarian Fried Rice   75

Khao Phad Pu (Thai Crab Fried Rice)   76

Khao Phad Goong (Thai Shrimp Fried Rice)   77

Khao Phad Talay (Thai Seafood Fried Rice)   77

Khao Phad Suparod (Thai Pineapple Fried Rice)   78

Khao Phad Kraprao Kai (Rice With Spicy Chicken and Basil)   80

Khao Phad Kraprao Goong (Rice With Spicy Shrimps and Basil)   81

Khao Khlook Kapi (Thai Fried Rice with Shrimp Paste
and Sweet Chicken)   82

To prepare rice, wash and drain 1 cup/ 250 mL of rice and cook with 1$\frac{1}{2}$ cups/375 mL of water in a covered pot for 15 minutes, or in a rice steamer. One cup/250 mL of raw rice yields 2$\frac{1}{2}$ cups/625 mL of cooked rice.

Khao Phad Kai
(Thai Chicken Fried Rice)

2½ cups	cooked rice	625 mL
6 oz	skinless, boneless chicken breast	175 g
6 tbsp	vegetable oil	75 mL
1 tsp	chopped garlic	5 mL
2	eggs	2
1 tbsp	fish sauce	15 mL
2 tbsp	soya sauce	25 mL
1 tbsp	oyster sauce	15 mL
½ tsp	black pepper	2 mL
2 tbsp	green peas (frozen)	25 mL

smells like dirty socks (Steve)

Strips of red pepper
Fresh coriander leaves
Slices of tomato and cucumber
Young Thailand Hot Sauce

*Serves 4 as a rice course or
2 as a main course.*

The closest Thai cookery comes to the Chinese is in its treatment of fried rice, with the obvious exception of the additional condiments that enhance with the particular flavours and tastes of Thailand.

1. Prepare 2½ cups/625 mL cooked rice (*page 73*). Reserve.
2. Slice the chicken into ¼-inch/5-mm strips. If you find it difficult to cut thinly through fresh meat, leave it in the freezer for 15-20 minutes to harden slightly and then slice. Reserve.
3. Heat oil in a wok (or large frying pan) until it is just about to smoke. Add garlic and stir-fry for 30 seconds. Add chicken and stir-fry for 1 minute. Turn heat down to medium and stir-fry for 1-2 minutes more, until the chicken has warmed through and turned white. Break the eggs directly into the wok. Increase heat to medium-high and fry the eggs without breaking them up for 2 minutes, until they're partially set.
4. Push the eggs and chicken to one side of the wok and add the rice to the other side. Add fish sauce, soya sauce and oyster sauce on the rice and then, using a shovelling motion, combine the two sides of the wok, tossing-stirring for 2 minutes, mixing the rice with the eggs and chicken, working from the bottom up, so that all the rice has a chance to fry in the oil, and everything is integrated.
5. Sprinkle black pepper on the rice and add green peas. Toss-stir for another minute, folding the peas into the rice and then remove from heat. Transfer to a serving dish and top with red pepper strips and fresh coriander leaves. Garnish sides with slices of tomato and cucumber and serve immediately with a side bowl of Young Thailand Hot Sauce (*page 37*).

Vegetarian Fried Rice

This easy and delectable recipe has the distinction of being entirely vegetarian and could become vegan if one omits the eggs. Naturally one need not be vegetarian to enjoy it. It's wonderful on its own, but it's unassuming enough to complement main course meat and fish dishes with the kind of interesting side tastes that plain steamed rice cannot offer.

1. Prepare 2½ cups/625 mL cooked rice *(page 73)*. Reserve.
2. Heat oil in a wok (or large frying pan) until it is just about to smoke. Add garlic and stir-fry for 30 seconds. Add mushrooms, carrots and broccoli and stir-fry for 1-2 minutes, until they have begun to warm through. Break the eggs directly into the wok and fry them without breaking them up for 2 minutes, until they are partially set.
3. Push the eggs and vegetables to one side of the wok and add rice to the other side. Add soya sauce on the rice and then using a shovelling motion, combine the two sides of the wok, tossing-stirring for 2 minutes, mixing the rice with the eggs and vegetables, working from the bottom up so that all the rice has a chance to fry in the oil and everything is integrated.
4. Sprinkle black pepper on the rice and add green peas. Toss-stir for another minute, folding the peas into the rice and then remove from heat. Transfer to a serving dish and top with red pepper strips and fresh coriander leaves. Garnish sides with slices of tomato and cucumber and serve immediately with a side bowl of Young Thailand Hot Sauce *(page 37)*.

2½ cups	cooked rice	625 mL
6 tbsp	vegetable oil	75 mL
1 tsp	garlic	5 mL
¼ cup	thinly sliced mushrooms (¼ inch/5 mm)	50 mL
¼ cup	finely cubed carrot (¼ inch/5 mm)	50 mL
½ cup	finely chopped broccoli florets (¼ inch/5 mm)	125 mL
2	eggs	2
3 tbsp	soya sauce	45 mL
½ tsp	black pepper	2 mL
2 tbsp	green peas (frozen)	25 mL

Strips of red pepper
Fresh coriander leaves
Slices of tomato and cucumber
Young Thailand Hot Sauce

Serves 2-4.

Khao Phad Pu
(Thai Crab Fried Rice)

2½ cups	cooked rice	625 mL
4 oz	crab meat	125 g
	(frozen, pre-cooked)	
8	crab claws	8
	(frozen, pre-cooked)	
6 tbsp	vegetable oil	75 mL
1 tsp	chopped garlic	5 mL
2	eggs	2
3 tbsp	soya sauce	45 mL
1 tsp	fish sauce	5 mL
1 tbsp	oyster sauce	15 mL
½ tsp	black pepper	2 mL
2 tbsp	green peas (frozen)	25 mL
1	stem green onion, thinly chopped	1

A thoroughly enjoyable rice that uses two kinds of crab: claws for munching and eye appeal, as well as crab meat which incorporates itself into the rice, flavouring it through and through. Variations of fried rice using other seafoods follow this recipe.

1. Prepare 2½ cups/625 mL cooked rice *(page 73)*. Reserve.
2. Squeeze excess water from the thawed crab meat. Reserve. Wash crab claws and reserve separately.
3. Heat oil in a wok (or large frying pan) until it is just about to smoke. Add garlic and stir-fry for 30 seconds. Add crab claws and stir-fry for 1 minute. Add crab meat and stir-fry for 30 seconds, breaking up the meat slightly. Decrease the heat to medium-high and break the eggs directly into the wok. Fry the eggs without breaking them up for 2 minutes, until they're partially set.
4. Push the eggs and crab to one side of the wok and add the rice to the other side. Add soya sauce, fish sauce and oyster sauce onto the rice, and then using a shovelling motion, combine the two sides of the wok, tossing-stirring for 2 minutes, mixing the rice with the eggs and crab, working from the bottom up, so that all the rice has a chance to fry in the oil and everything is integrated.
5. Sprinkle black pepper on the rice and add green peas and green onions. Toss-stir for another minute, folding the peas into the rice and then remove from heat. Transfer to a serving dish and top with red pepper strips and fresh coriander

Strips of red pepper
Fresh coriander leaves
Wedges of lime
Slices of tomato and cucumber
YOUNG THAILAND Hot Sauce

*Serves 4 as a rice course or
2 as a main course.*

leaves. Garnish sides with lime wedges and slices of tomato and cucumber. Serve immediately with a side bowl of YOUNG THAILAND Hot Sauce *(page 37)*.

Variations:

Khao Phad Goong (Thai Shrimp Fried Rice). Replace the crab of the above recipe with 16 large shrimps, shelled and deveined, stir-frying all of them at once in step #3 for 1 minute and proceeding with the recipe.

Khao Phad Talay (Thai Seafood Fried Rice). Replace the crab of the above recipe with a combination of: 4 shelled mussels; 8 large shrimps, shelled and deveined; 4 oz/125 g cleaned squid, sliced into 1/2-inch/1-cm rings; and 4 frozen, pre-cooked crab claws. Stir-fry all these seafoods at once in step #3 for 1 minute and proceed with the recipe.

Khao Phad Suparod
(Thai Pineapple Fried Rice)

2½ cups	cooked rice	625 mL
4 oz	skinless, boneless chicken breast	125 g
8	large shrimps, shelled and deveined (5 oz/150 g)	8
	Top half of a small pineapple	
6 tbsp	vegetable oil	75 mL
1 tsp	chopped garlic	5 mL
2	eggs	2
3 tbsp	soya sauce	45 mL
2 tbsp	fish sauce	25 mL
½ tsp	black pepper	2 mL
⅓ cup	roasted unsalted cashews	75 mL
2	stems green onion, thinly chopped	2

Strips of red pepper
Fresh coriander leaves
Slices of tomato and cucumber
Young Thailand Hot Sauce

Serves 2-4.

Here's one that'll please everyone and especially the kids. Mild in flavour, it's loaded with treats: shrimps, pineapple, cashew nuts, chicken. Colourful and pleasant, it's ideal for a festive summer lunch or, even better, for evoking summer on a bleak winter's eve.

1. Prepare 2½ cups/625 mL cooked rice *(page 73)*. Reserve.
2. Slice the chicken into ¼-inch/5-mm strips. If you find it difficult to cut thinly through fresh meat, leave it in the freezer for 15-20 minutes to harden slightly and then slice. Reserve along with the shrimps.
3. Cut a small pineapple in half horizontally. Reserve the bottom half for dessert. Peel the top half and then slice vertically into quarters. Cut out the triangle of core from each quarter and discard. Slice the cleaned pineapple into ½-inch/1-cm pieces. Reserve.
4. Heat oil in a wok (or large frying pan) until it is just about to smoke. Add garlic and stir-fry for 30 seconds. Add chicken and shrimps and stir-fry for 1-1½ minutes, until the meats have turned white, then decrease heat to medium-high. Break the eggs directly into the wok. Fry the eggs without breaking them up for 2 minutes, until they are partially set.
5. Push the eggs and meats to one side of the wok, and add the rice to the other side. Add soya sauce and fish sauce on the rice and then using a shovelling motion, combine the two sides of the wok, tossing-stirring for 2 minutes, mixing the rice with the eggs, chicken and shrimp, working from the bottom up so that all the rice has a chance to fry in the oil and everything is integrated.

THE YOUNG THAILAND COOKBOOK

6. Sprinkle black pepper on the rice and add cashews, green onion and the reserved pineapple chunks. Toss-stir for 1-1½ minutes, folding the new ingredients into the rice and then remove from heat. Transfer to a serving dish and top with red pepper strips and fresh coriander leaves. Garnish sides with slices of tomato and cucumber. Serve immediately with a side bowl of YOUNG THAILAND Hot Sauce *(page 37)*.

A note on pineapple: you'll need half of a small fruit for the pineapple require-ments of this recipe. Wandee recom-mends that one use the top half of the fruit for cooking, reserving the bottom half for dessert: apparently the bottom half is always sweeter, something to do with fruit sugar developing below and then rising to the top. I tested her theory on ten pineapples and it worked with every one. Live and learn.

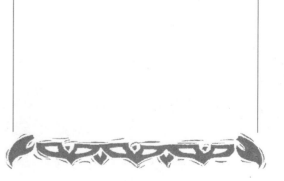

Khao Phad Kraprao Kai (Rice With Spicy Chicken and Basil)

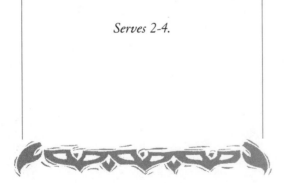

2 1/2 cups	cooked rice	625 mL
8 oz	skinless, boneless chicken breast	250 g
1/2	medium red pepper	1/2
1/2	medium green pepper	1/2
5 tbsp	vegetable oil	70 mL
1 tbsp	chopped garlic	15 mL
4	fresh hot chilies, finely chopped	4
3 tbsp	soya sauce	45 mL
2 tbsp	fish sauce	25 mL
1 tsp	sugar	5 mL
1/3 cup	water	75 mL
20	whole leaves fresh basil	20
1/2 tsp	cornstarch	2 mL
1 tbsp	water	15 mL

Young Thailand Hot Sauce

Serves 2-4.

Steamed, comforting rice, topped with a saucy stir-fry of chicken, peppers and basil leaves, is both exciting and familiar. Reminiscent of "rice and" recipes of a number of cuisines and especially the Chinese, it allows an alternative to fried rice and feels more like a proper meal. Being Thai, it naturally offers a good range of complementary flavours and so it appears delicate and exotic, while being basic and hearty. It's also very easy to make. An overall good choice for dining companions of varying appetites and tastes. A version using shrimps is noted at the end of this recipe.

1. Cook 1 cup/250 mL of Thai Jasmin rice with 1 1/2 cups/375 mL water to prepare 2 1/2 cups/625 mL of cooked rice. While the rice cooks, proceed with the preparation of the stir-fry which will be the topping.
2. Slice the chicken into 1/4-inch/5-mm strips. If you find it difficult to cut thinly through fresh meat, leave it in the freezer for 15-20 minutes to harden slightly and then slice. Reserve.
3. Chop the red and green peppers into 1-inch/2.5-cm squares. Reserve.
4. Heat oil in a wok (or frying pan) until it is just about to smoke. Add garlic and chilies and stir-fry for 30 seconds. Add chicken strips and stir-fry for 2 minutes. Add soya sauce, fish sauce, sugar and water and stir-fry for another 2 minutes. Add red and green pepper squares and 3/4 of the basil leaves, stir and let cook for 2-3 minutes, until the peppers have just begun to soften.

5. Check your rice, which should be ready. Remove from fire and reserve in its cooking pot, covered.
6. Dissolve cornstarch in 1 tbsp/15 mL cold water in a small bowl. Add to the stir-fry in the wok. Reduce the fire to low and cook, stirring for less than a minute. The sauce around the meat will thicken somewhat. Take off the fire and cover.
7. Fluff the rice and transfer to a serving dish. Place the chicken stir-fry with all its sauce on top of the rice. Decorate with the remaining basil leaves and serve immediately, accompanied by a side bowl of Young Thailand Hot Sauce (page 37).

Variation:

Khao Phad Kraprao Goong (Rice With Spicy Shrimps and Basil):
Replace the chicken in this recipe with 12 large shrimps, shelled and deveined. Stir-fry the shrimps for only 1 minute (instead of 2) in step #4, when they are first added to the oil/garlic/chilies in the wok; then after adding soya sauce, fish sauce, sugar and water, again stir-fry for 1 minute, instead of 2. Proceed with the recipe.

Khao Khlook Kapi (Thai Fried Rice with Shrimp Paste and Sweet Chicken)

2 1/2 cups	cooked rice	625 mL
4 tbsp	vegetable oil	50 mL
1 tsp	garlic	5 mL
1 tsp	shrimp paste	5 mL
2 tbsp	warm water	25 mL
1 tbsp	fish sauce	15 mL
2 tbsp	dried shrimps	25 mL
4 tbsp	vegetable oil	50 mL
1 tsp	chopped garlic	5 mL
1/2	small onion, roughly chopped	1/2
4 oz	skinless, boneless chicken breast in 1/2-inch/1-cm strips	125 g
2 tbsp	soya sauce	25 mL
1/2 tsp	black pepper	2 mL
1 tbsp	sugar	15 mL
2 tbsp	rice (or white) wine	25 mL
1 tbsp	fish sauce	15 mL
1 tbsp	vegetable oil	15 mL
2	eggs	2

If any recipe could be considered the original Thai fried rice, this would have to be it. Invented for the royal court, it combines a shrimp-flavoured rice with a sweetened chicken stir-fry and scrambled eggs on top: a construct of an old and gracious world, where pleasures were enjoyed in turn, instead of mixed together as in the fried rice of today.

This recipe calls for three operations to be executed quickly, one after the other, so that the fried rice of the first procedure is still warm when the egg of the third has been fried to top it, having already waited through the stir-frying of the chicken in the middle.

Is this authentic, rarely seen dish worth all the fuss? Absolutely! Not only is it delicious, it affords a sense of accomplishment when it finally arrives at the table.

1. Prepare 2 1/2 cups/625 mL cooked rice *(page 73)*. Reserve.
2. Chop the onion and chicken for the stir-fry and reserve.
3. Heat 4 tbsp/50 mL oil in a wok (or large frying pan) until it is just about to smoke. Add garlic and stir-fry for 30 seconds. Dissolve shrimp paste in warm water and add to wok along with fish sauce. Stir-cook for less than a minute, until bubbling hard. Add dried shrimps and stir-fry for 30 seconds. Add rice, then using a shovelling motion, stir-fry the rice for 2-3 minutes, tossing-stirring from the bottom up, so that all

the rice has a chance to fry in the oil and all the ingredients are thoroughly integrated. Transfer to a serving dish and cover, while you tackle the next step.

4. Heat 4 tbsp/50 mL oil in another wok (or frying pan). Add garlic and stir-fry for 30 seconds. Add chopped onion and stir-fry for 1 minute. Add chicken strips and stir-fry for 1 more minute. Then, in quick succession, add (sprinkling evenly over the chicken) soya sauce, black pepper, sugar, wine and fish sauce. Continue stir-frying for another 2 minutes until the chicken appears shiny and cooked. Transfer to the side of the fried rice in the serving dish. Cover again.

5. Heat 1 tbsp/15 mL of oil in a frying pan. Beat the eggs lightly in a bowl. Add to the oil and fry them for 2-3 minutes, pulling them in from the sides, in a manner that would be a cross between omelette and scrambled. Do not overcook. Take off the fire and break up into large chunks. Top the rice with this egg. Decorate the egg with red pepper strips, onion slices and fresh coriander leaves. Garnish the sides with slices of cucumber and lime wedges. Serve immediately with a side bowl of YOUNG THAILAND Hot Sauce *(page 37)*.

Strips of red pepper
Thinly sliced red onion
Fresh coriander leaves
Slices of cucumber
Wedges of lime
YOUNG THAILAND Hot Sauce

Serves 2-4

Wandee creates the flavourful collage lightning fast, using only one wok, which she found time to clean after each step before proceeding to the next. For more timid chefs like myself, it is prudent to have three frying implements at the ready and to also prepare all the ingredients of the chicken stir-fry in advance, lined up and eager to be used when their number is called.

BEEF

Nuer Num Mun Hoy (Beef with Oyster Sauce and Mushrooms) 86

Nuer Phad Phed (Thai Spicy Beef) 87

Nuer Nam Tok (Spicy Beef Salad) 88

Nuer Yang (Marinated Grilled Beef) 89

Panang Nuer (Beef in Thick Coconut Milk Sauce) 90

Kang Ped Nuer (Thai Beef Curry) 91

Kang Masaman Nuer (Thai Beef Sweet and Sour Curry) 92

Nuer Num Mun Hoy (Beef with Oyster Sauce and Mushrooms)

10 oz	trimmed beef flank steak	300 g
5 tbsp	vegetable oil	70 mL
1 tsp	garlic	5 mL
½	small white onion, roughly chopped	½
4 oz	mushrooms, quartered	125 g
2 tbsp	oyster sauce	25 mL
2 tbsp	water	25 mL
1 tsp	sugar	5 mL
½ tsp	black pepper	2 mL
1 tbsp	rice (or white) wine	15 mL
2	stems green onion, in 1-inch/2.5-cm pieces	2
1 tsp	cornstarch	5 mL
1 tbsp	cold water	15 mL

Strips of red pepper
Fresh coriander leaves
Slices of tomato

2½ cups	freshly steamed rice	625 mL

Serves 4.

Beef cookery is a relative newcomer to Thai cuisine, as the indigenous Buddhist culture abstains from the meat of the holy cows. It is the Chinese and Moslem communities of Thailand that have contributed the beef recipes, and we start with a soothing stir-fry that has its origins in China.

1. Slice the steak into pieces that are ¼ inch/5 mm thick, 2 inches/5 cm long and about 1 inch/2.5 cm wide. If you find it difficult to cut thinly through fresh meat, leave it in the freezer for 15-20 minutes to harden slightly and then slice. Reserve.

2. Heat oil in a wok (or large frying pan) on high heat until it is just about to smoke. Add garlic and stir-fry for 30 seconds. Add onion, mushrooms, beef and oyster sauce and stir-fry for 2 minutes, until everything is sizzling in the oil. Add water and stir-fry for 30 seconds. Add sugar and black pepper and stir-fry for about 1½ minutes, until it all looks ready to eat.

3. Add wine, green onion and the dissolved cornstarch. Stir-fry for another minute as the sauce thickens somewhat around the meat. Transfer to a serving dish and top with red pepper strips and coriander leaves. Garnish the sides with slices of tomato and serve immediately, accompanied by steamed rice.

Nuer Phad Phed
(Thai Spicy Beef)

Colourful vegetables, basil leaves, tender steak and red curry paste: an irresistible combination for fans of red meat, in a recipe that is fast and easy, but produces a result that impresses with its complex tastes and varied textures.

1. Slice the steak into pieces that are ¼ inch/5 mm thick, 2 inches/5 cm long and about 1 inch/2.5 cm wide. If you find it difficult to cut thinly through fresh meat, leave it in the freezer for 15-20 minutes to harden slightly and then slice. Reserve.
2. Cut red and green peppers into 1-inch/2.5-cm squares. Trim ends of the long beans and chop into 1-inch/2.5-cm pieces. Reserve peppers and beans together.
3. Heat oil in a wok (or large frying pan) on high heat until it is just about to smoke. Add garlic and curry paste and stir-fry for about 45 seconds. Immediately add coconut milk (or water) and lime leaves. Stir-cook for 1-2 minutes, until it's bubbling and thick.
4. Add beef, bamboo shoots, peppers and long beans all at once. Stir-fry for 1 minute, making sure that everything fries in the oil as you're stirring. Add fish sauce and sugar and stir-fry for 2-3 minutes, until the peppers have softened some-what and the beef has browned. Add ¾ of the basil leaves and stir-fry for one more minute.
5. Transfer to a serving dish and top with red pepper strips and the remaining basil leaves. Serve immediately, accompanied by steamed rice.

10 oz	trimmed beef flank steak	300 g
¼	medium green pepper	¼
¼	medium red pepper	¼
6	long green beans	6
5 tbsp	vegetable oil	70 mL
1 tsp	chopped garlic	5 mL
2 tbsp	red curry paste	25 mL
5 tbsp	unsweetened coconut milk (or water)	70 mL
2	lime leaves, torn into thirds	2
½ cup	bamboo shoot strips	125 mL
2 tbsp	fish sauce	25 mL
1 tbsp	sugar	15 mL
20	fresh basil leaves	20
	Strips of red pepper	
2½ cups	freshly steamed rice	625 mL

Serves 4.

Nuer Nam Tok
(Spicy Beef Salad)

10 oz	trimmed beef flank steak	300 g
4 tbsp	lime juice	50 mL
2 tbsp	fish sauce	25 mL
1 tsp	sugar	5 mL
¼ tsp	roasted chilies	1 mL
2 tbsp	roughly chopped coriander	25 mL
2 tbsp	roughly chopped mint	25 mL
1	stem green onion, finely chopped	1
½	medium red pepper, in thin strips	½
½	small red onion, thinly sliced	½
1 tbsp	spicy rice (optional)	15 mL

Strips of red pepper
Fresh coriander leaves
Slices of cucumber
Wedges of lime
Four long green beans
Vegetarian Fried Rice (optional)

Serves 4.

This is a very easy, very appealing recipe that makes a lovely lunch in summer and works as part of a party buffet any time of year. It takes mere minutes to prepare and assemble and becomes even better if it has to wait before being served. "Accommodating" is its middle name.

1. Slice the steak into pieces that are ¼ inch/5 mm thick, 2 inches/5 cm long and about 1 inch/2.5 cm wide. If you find it difficult to cut thinly through fresh meat, leave it in the freezer for 15-20 minutes to harden slightly and then slice.

2. Grill/broil or bake (in 450°F/230°C oven) the steak slices for 2 minutes each side (a little longer for "medium"). Transfer to a work bowl.

3. In a separate bowl beat lime juice, fish sauce, sugar and roasted chilies *(page 40)*, until blended. Add to the meat and mix to coat. Add herbs, green onion, red pepper and red onion. Mix again to integrate. Add spicy rice (if using) and mix to evenly distribute.

4. Transfer to a serving dish and top with red pepper strips and coriander leaves. Garnish the sides with cucumber slices and lime wedges. Trim long beans and cut into 2-inch/5-cm pieces. Place beans decoratively on a corner of the salad. Now ready, the salad can be served immediately or it can wait for up to 1½ hours, unrefrigerated and lightly covered. Serve along with Vegetarian Fried Rice *(page 75)* if a main course item.

Nuer Yang
(Marinated Grilled Beef)

Be it beef, chicken or pork, marinated meat on the grill is for many people the very definition of summer. That and beer which happens to be the best (arguably, the only) way to wash down this tasty grill and its accompanying Thai signature Cucumber Salad and Hot Sauce. This recipe calls for beef but one could use exactly the same method for chicken or pork.

1. Slice the steak into pieces that are ¼ inch/5 mm thick, 2 inches/5 cm long and about 1 inch/2.5 cm wide. If you find it difficult to cut thinly through fresh meat, leave it in the freezer for 15-20 minutes to harden slightly, and then slice. Transfer meat slices to a work bowl.
2. In a separate bowl beat soya sauce, garlic, black pepper, sugar and oil to blend. Add to the meat and mix to coat. Leave to marinate, unrefrigerated, for 10-15 minutes (not longer, as that would over-soften the meat).
3. Grill (or broil) the marinated steak slices for 2 minutes each side (a little longer for "medium"). Transfer to a serving dish and top with red pepper strips and fresh coriander leaves. Garnish the sides with tomato slices and lime wedges. Serve immediately, accompanied by Cucumber Salad *(page 23)* and YOUNG THAILAND Hot Sauce *(page 37)*.

10 oz	trimmed beef flank steak	300 g
1 tbsp	soya sauce	15 mL
1 tbsp	chopped garlic	15 mL
½ tsp	black pepper	2 mL
½ tsp	sugar	2 mL
1 tsp	vegetable oil	5 mL

Strips of red pepper
Fresh coriander leaves
Slices of tomato
Wedges of lime
Cucumber Salad
YOUNG THAILAND Hot Sauce

Serves 4.

10 oz	trimmed beef flank steak	300 g
2	lime leaves	2
2 cups	unsweetened coconut milk	500 mL
2 tbsp	red curry paste	25 mL
1 tbsp	fish sauce	15 mL
2 tbsp	ground roasted unsalted peanuts	25 mL
1 tbsp	sugar	15 mL
¼	small red onion, finely sliced	¼
	Some fresh basil leaves	
2½ cups	freshly steamed rice	625 mL

Serves 4.

Thai cuisine uses a lot of coconut milk in curry sauces, but this one is special because it is cooked longer, until the sauce is reduced down to its addictive essence. And therein lies the catch: if over-reduced, the sauce becomes too spare. But no matter. The situation can be remedied with some fresh coconut milk (or water) and a couple of stirs.

Panang Nuer (Beef in Thick Coconut Milk Sauce)

Melting beef in the embrace of a thickened coconut milk-red curry-ground peanut cloud; breezily perfumed with lime leaf; rich, bright, intensely pleasurable…have I made it plain that I love this dish?

1. Slice the steak into pieces that are ¼ inch/5 mm thick, 2 inches/5 cm long and about 1 inch/2.5 cm wide. If you find it difficult to cut meat thinly, put it in the freezer for 15-20 minutes to harden slightly and then slice. Reserve.
2. Thinly slice the lime leaves (with a very sharp, heavy knife). Reserve.
3. Heat 1 cup/250 mL of the coconut milk in a wok (or frying pan) and add the red curry paste. Stir to dissolve and cook at high heat for 5-6 minutes, until the oil of the coconut rises to the top and the sauce is thick. Add fish sauce and stir it in.
4. Immediately add the second cup of coconut milk and the reserved beef. Reduce heat to medium-high and stir-cook for 1 minute. Add the ground peanuts, ¾ of the reserved lime leaf shreds and the sugar. Stir. Turn heat back to maximum and cook for 8-10 minutes, stirring occasionally, until the liquids have reduced (it'll be a red-brown, thick mantle covering the meat generously but with not much to spare).
5. Reduce heat to medium-low and let simmer for 3-4 minutes while the oil of the coconut again rises to the top. Take off heat and transfer to a serving dish. Top with the rest of the shredded lime leaf, the onion slices and the basil leaves. Serve immediately, accompanied by steamed rice.

Kang Ped Nuer
(Thai Beef Curry)

This coconut-milk based, saucy beef is totally foolproof. Unlike the last recipe, it has lots of sauce at the end (even though it uses only 3 tbsp/45 mL more liquid) and requires a lot less cooking. The beef is partnered with strips of bamboo shoot and though still spicy, it has the kind of comfort one finds in a mild Indian curry.

1. Slice the steak into pieces that are ¼ inch/5 mm thick, 2 inches/5 cm long and about 1 inch/2.5 cm wide. If you find it difficult to cut thinly through fresh meat, leave it in the freezer for 15-20 minutes to harden slightly and then slice. Reserve.
2. Heat 1 cup/250 mL of the coconut milk in a wok (or frying pan) and add the red curry paste. Stir to dissolve and cook at high heat for 5-6 minutes, until the oil of the coconut milk rises to the top and the sauce is thick. Add fish sauce and stir it in.
3. Immediately add the second cup of coconut milk and the reserved beef. Reduce heat to medium. Tear the lime leaves in thirds and add to the wok. Stir-cook for 30 seconds. Add the bamboo shoot strips and the sugar. Return the heat to maximum and add 3 tbsp/45 mL water. Cook, stirring for 3 minutes until nicely bubbling. Add ¾ of the basil leaves, the red pepper strips and the green peas. Stir and cook for another 30 seconds, folding all the ingredients into the sauce.
4. Take off heat and transfer to a serving dish. Top with the rest of the basil leaves and the additional red pepper strips. Serve immediately, accompanied by steamed rice.

10 oz	trimmed beef flank steak	300 g
2 cups	unsweetened coconut milk	500 mL
2 tbsp	red curry paste	25 mL
1 tsp	fish sauce	5 mL
2	lime leaves	2
1 cup	bamboo shoot strips	250 mL
1 tsp	sugar	5 mL
3 tbsp	water	45 mL
20	leaves of fresh basil	20
¼	medium red pepper, in thin strips	¼
2 tbsp	green peas (frozen)	25 mL

Additional strips of red pepper
| 2½ cups | freshly steamed rice | 625 mL |

Serves 4.

Kang Masaman Nuer
(Thai Beef Sweet and Sour Curry)

2 tbsp	tamarind paste	25 mL
2 tbsp	warm water	25 mL
10 oz	trimmed beef flank steak	300 g
3 cups	unsweetened coconut milk	750 mL
2 tbsp	red curry paste	25 mL
2 tbsp	masaman curry paste	25 mL
1/2	medium onion, roughly chopped	1/2
1 tbsp	fish sauce	15 mL
3 tsp	sugar	15 mL
2 tbsp	roasted unsalted peanuts	25 mL
	Strips of red pepper	
2 1/2 cups	freshly steamed rice	625 mL

Serves 4.

Another cousin of the Panang Nuer, *this addictive number is just as aromatic and pleasurable, while being much easier to achieve, because it has a full-bodied sauce with none of the tricky sauce-reduction of its relative.*

1. Combine tamarind paste and warm water in a small bowl and let soak for at least 15 minutes. Reserve.
2. Slice the steak in 1/2-inch/1-cm cubes. Reserve.
3. Return to your reserved tamarind paste in its water. Mash it and transfer the mud-like mixture to a strainer set into a bowl. Mash and push with a spoon, forcing the liquid to strain into the bowl. Scrape off the juice that clings to the underside of the strainer. You will have about 2 tbsp/25 mL of tamarind juice. Reserve. Discard the solids left in the strainer.
4. Heat 2 cups/500mL of the coconut milk in a wok (or frying pan) on maximum heat to boiling. Add red curry and masaman curry pastes and stir to dissolve. Add beef, mix, then add onions, mixing again. Cook for 3-4 minutes until happily bubbling, stirring once in a while.
5. Add reserved tamarind juice, fish sauce and sugar. Stir and cook for 2-3 minutes until bubbling strongly. Turn heat down to medium and cook for 15-20 minutes, stirring occasionally, until the oil of the coconut has risen to the surface and the beef is quite tender.

THE YOUNG THAILAND COOKBOOK

6. Add the third cup of coconut milk and the peanuts. Raise heat to maximum and cook, stirring often for 3-4 minutes, until the oil has once again risen to the surface. Take off heat and transfer to a serving dish. Top with strips of red pepper and serve immediately, accompanied by steamed rice.

The sauce, derived from North Indian Moslem cookery (masaman is a corruption of the word "Musalman" or "Moslem"), is sweet and sour rather than hot, using a combination of two kinds of curry paste, as well as tamarind.

Many Thai chefs make this curry with potato. Add 1 cup/250 mL of peeled potatoes cut into 1/2-inch/1-cm cubes, along with the onions, in step #4. Proceed with the recipe.

Chicken

Kai Hima Parn
(Cashew Nut Chicken)

10 oz	skinless, boneless chicken breast	300 g
½	medium red pepper	½
½	orange	½
3 tbsp	vegetable oil	45 mL
1 tsp	chopped garlic	5 mL
1 tbsp	soya sauce	15 mL
1 tsp	lime juice	5 mL
2 tbsp	chili paste	25 mL
⅔ cup	roasted unsalted cashews	150 mL
	Fresh coriander leaves	
2½ cups	freshly steamed rice	625 mL

Serves 4.

Orange rind is yet another of the inedible items that Thai culinary sensibility leaves in the finished product. Unlike lemon grass, galangal root and lime leaves, it is attached to an edible substance. How one spits out the rind, after having eaten the orange, I leave to the ingenuity of the eater.

This sunny, gently spiced dish kicks off this section devoted entirely to the sweetly succulent (if cooked right) chicken breast meat, an ingredient that seems to be included in some fashion in a great number of Thai offerings.

1. Slice the chicken into strips that are ¼ inch/5 mm thick, 2 inch/5 cm long and about 1 inch/2.5 cm wide. If you find it difficult to cut thinly through fresh meat, leave it in the freezer for 15-20 minutes to harden slightly, and then slice. Reserve.
2. Cut the pepper into 1-inch/2.5-cm squares. Reserve. Cut the orange in half vertically and then slice into ½-inch/1-cm wide wedges. Cut the wedges down to ½-inch/1-cm chunks. Reserve.
3. Heat oil in a wok (or large frying pan) on high heat until it is just about to smoke. Add garlic and stir-fry for 30 seconds. Add reserved chicken and soya sauce and stir-fry for 2 minutes, until the chicken has started to turn white and the oil sizzles around it.
4. Add lime juice and stir-fry for 30 seconds. Add reserved orange and pepper pieces, as well as the chili paste, and stir-fry for 30 seconds to distribute evenly. Add cashew nuts and stir-fry for 1 minute, until everything is mixed together, shiny and appears ready to eat. Transfer to a serving dish, top with fresh coriander leaves and serve immediately, accompanied by steamed rice.

THE YOUNG THAILAND COOKBOOK

Kai Kraphao (Basil Chicken)

A spicy, basil-perfumed sauce around tender chicken and crunchy peppers: a delightful companion for steamed rice that is executed in mere minutes. This one is for those occasions when the desire to please need not be compromised by a tight schedule.

10 oz	skinless, boneless chicken breast	300 g
1/2	medium red or green pepper	1/2
5 tbsp	vegetable oil	70 mL
1 tsp	chopped garlic	5 mL
6	fresh hot chilies, roughly chopped	6
1 tbsp	fish sauce	15 mL
1 tsp	sugar	5 mL
1 tbsp	soya sauce	15 mL
1 tbsp	oyster sauce	15 mL
2 tbsp	water	25 mL
20	whole leaves fresh basil	20
1/2 tsp	cornstarch	2 mL
1 tbsp	water	15 mL
2 1/2 cups	freshly steamed rice	625 mL

Serves 4.

1. Slice the chicken into strips that are 1/4 inch/5-mm thick, 2 inch/5 cm long and about 1 inch/2.5 cm wide. If you find it difficult to cut meat thinly, put it in the freezer for 15-20 minutes to harden slightly, and then slice. Reserve.

2. Cut the pepper into 1-inch/2.5-cm squares. Reserve.

3. Heat oil in a wok (or large frying pan) on high heat until it is just about to smoke. Add garlic and chilies and stir-fry for 30 seconds. Add reserved chicken and stir-fry for 2 minutes. Add fish sauce, sugar and soya sauce and stir-fry for 1 minute. Add oyster sauce and water and cook for 30 seconds.

4. Add reserved peppers and 3/4 of the basil leaves and stir-fry for 2 minutes until the peppers have begun to soften. Dissolve cornstarch in water, add to wok and stir-fry for 1 minute, until the sauce has thickened somewhat. Take off fire and transfer to a serving dish. Top with the remainder of the basil and serve, immediately accompanied by steamed rice.

Variation:

Moo Kraphao (Basil Pork): You can substitute 10 oz/300 g of trimmed pork tenderloin for the chicken content of this recipe, proceeding exactly otherwise, to create *Moo Kraphao* (Basil Pork).

Kai Phad Khing
(Ginger Chicken)

This mild dish, perfumed and tender, is like a sea breeze on a steamy, tropical night. Very lightly flavoured, it derives its exotic character from the plentiful ginger, which acts both as vegetable and condiment.

10 oz	skinless, boneless chicken breast	300 g
2 inches	ginger root	5 cm
5 tbsp	vegetable oil	70 mL
1 tsp	chopped garlic	5 mL
2 tbsp	soya sauce	25 mL
4 oz	mushrooms, thinly sliced	125 g
1/4 cup	water	50 mL
1 tbsp	oyster sauce	15 mL
1 tsp	sugar	5 mL
1/2 tsp	black pepper	2 mL
1/2	medium onion, roughly chopped	1/2
1	stem green onion in 1-inch/2.5-cm pieces	1
1/2 tsp	cornstarch	2 mL
1 tbsp	water	15 mL

Pinch black pepper
Strips of red pepper
Fresh coriander leaves

2 1/2 cups	freshly steamed rice	625 mL

Serves 4.

1. Slice the chicken into strips that are 1/4 inch/5 mm thick, 2 inch/5 cm long and about 1 inch/2.5 cm wide. If you find it difficult to cut thinly through fresh meat, leave it in the freezer for 15-20 minutes to harden slightly, and then slice. Reserve.

2. Peel the ginger root and cut into 1/8-inch/2.5-mm thick rounds. Stack a few rounds at a time and chop thinly to make shreds. Repeat until all the ginger has been shredded. Place the shreds in a strainer and run them under cold water. Drain and reserve.

3. Heat oil in a wok (or large frying pan) on high heat until it is just about to smoke. Add chopped garlic and stir-fry for 30 seconds. Add reserved chicken and soya sauce and stir-fry for 2 minutes. Add reserved ginger shreds and mushrooms, along with 1/4 cup/50 mL water and stir-cook for 1 minute, until everything is integrated.

4. Add oyster sauce, sugar and black pepper and stir-fry for 2 minutes. Add onion and green onion and stir-fry for 1 minute. Dissolve cornstarch in water, add to wok and stir-fry for a final 30 seconds, until the sauce has thickened somewhat. Take off fire and transfer to a serving dish. Sprinkle black pepper, and top with red pepper strips and fresh coriander leaves. Serve immediately, accompanied by steamed rice.

Kai Yang
(Marinated Grilled Chicken)

This is yet another of the marvellous Thai grills, this time of entire chicken breasts that have been primed in an aromatic, sweet-salty marinade and cooked up fast and juicy to perk up any appetite.

1. Prepare chicken breasts by butterflying (cutting without detaching) the thicker ends, so that you end up with large, flat pieces about ½ inch/1 cm thick. Lay the chicken flat on a large plate. Sprinkle and spread marinating ingredients (garlic, soya sauce, black pepper, sugar and vegetable oil), so that the entire surface is covered. Turn the chicken over a few times to marinate both sides. Let it marinate for 3-5 minutes, unrefrigerated.
2. Grill/broil chicken for 3-4 minutes each side, until done (press with a finger: when it feels firm, it is done), and slightly charred all around.
3. Line the plate with lettuce leaves. Transfer the grilled chicken to a cutting board and slice it in ½-inch/1-cm strips. Transfer the strips onto the lettuce and top with red pepper strips and fresh coriander leaves. Serve immediately, accompanied by Young Thailand Hot Sauce *(page 37)*, Thai Sweet and Sour Sauce *(page 38)* and steamed rice.

24 oz	skinless, boneless chicken breast	750 g
1 tbsp	chopped garlic	15 mL
2 tbsp	soya sauce	25 mL
1 tsp	black pepper	5 mL
1 tbsp	sugar	15 mL
1 tbsp	vegetable oil	15 mL

Lettuce leaves
Slices of tomato and cucumber
Strips of red pepper
Fresh coriander leaves
Young Thailand Hot Sauce
Thai Sweet and Sour Sauce

2½ cups	freshly steamed rice	625 mL

Serves 4.

Kaeng Khiao Wan Kai (Chicken in Thai Green Curry)

10 oz	skinless, boneless chicken breast	300 g
3 cups	unsweetened coconut milk	750 mL
2 tbsp	green curry paste	25 mL
2	lime leaves	2
1 cup	water	250 mL
3 tbsp	fish sauce	45 mL
1 tsp	sugar	5 mL
1 cup	bamboo shoot strips	250 mL
1/2	medium red pepper, in thin strips	1/2
2 tbsp	green peas (frozen)	25 mL
20	whole leaves fresh basil	20

This is the one chicken dish that will leave them gasping (from the heat) while searching for more and more compliments to the chef. A simple, coconut-milk stew achieves mythic proportions when dressed up with lime leaves and the twelve-ingredient, extra-fiery Thai green curry paste. There are no special tricks in the preparation of this recipe, which ends up as a juicy, flavourful curry that needs lots of rice on the side, and a fire-extinguisher at the end.

1. Slice the chicken into strips that are 1/4 inch/5 mm thick, 2 inch/5 cm long and about 1 inch/2.5 cm wide. If you find it difficult to cut thinly through fresh meat, leave it in the freezer for 15-20 minutes to harden slightly, and then slice. Reserve.

2. Heat 1 cup/250 mL of the coconut milk in a wok (or large frying pan) on high heat, until it boils. Add green curry paste and, reducing the heat to medium, stir to dissolve it in the coconut milk. Add second cup of coconut milk, raise the heat to maximum and let cook for 8-10 minutes until the oil of the coconut milk rises to the top and the sauce thickens somewhat. Tear the lime leaves in thirds and add to the wok. Turn heat back to medium and cook for 2 minutes.

3. Add chicken, turn heat back to maximum. Stir chicken into the sauce and immediately add the third (and last) cup of coconut milk, as well as a cup of water. Stir-cook for 1 minute until the mixture is bubbling happily. Add fish sauce and sugar and stir-cook for 2 minutes, until it is bubbling hard.

Strips of red pepper
| 2½ cups | freshly | 625 mL |
| | steamed rice | |

4. Add bamboo shoots and stir-cook for 2 minutes. Add red pepper and stir-cook for 1 minute. Add green peas and ¾ of the basil leaves. Stir-cook for 1-2 minutes, folding the ingredients into the sauce, until it all seems ready to eat.
5. Take off heat and transfer into a deep serving dish. Top with some additional red pepper strips and the rest of the basil. Serve immediately, accompanied by steamed rice.

Serves 4.

This curry can be made in advance. It has lots of sauce which can be reheated quickly without too much loss of quality.

Larb Kai
(Thai Chicken Salad)

10 oz	skinless, boneless chicken breast	300 g
1	stem lemon grass	1
5 tbsp	water	70 mL
2 tbsp	fish sauce	25 mL
4 tbsp	lime juice	50 mL
½ tsp	roasted chilies	2 mL
2 tbsp	spicy rice (optional)	25 mL
1	stem green onion, thinly chopped	1
2 tbsp	roughly chopped fresh coriander	25 mL
4 tbsp	roughly chopped fresh mint	50 mL
½	medium red onion, thinly sliced	½
⅓	medium red pepper, in thin strips	⅓

Lettuce leaves
Additional fresh coriander leaves,
fresh mint leaves, red pepper strips
Wedges of lime
Slices of cucumber and tomato

Serves 4.

This is another one of the highly stylized Thai meat salads, which, like its relative, the pork-based Yum Naem Sod, makes a perfect light lunch in summer or, even better, a touch of exotica on a party buffet.

1. Place chicken on a board and, using a chef's knife, pound and chop until minced. Reserve. Smash lemon grass with the flat of a chef's knife once and then chop into 1-inch/2.5-cm pieces.

2. Heat 5 tbsp/70 mL water in a wok (or frying pan) on high heat. Add lemon grass pieces and let boil for 30 seconds. Add minced chicken and stir-cook for 2-3 minutes, until the chicken is cooked. Meanwhile the water will evaporate, but then the chicken will emit its own juice. Take off heat and transfer to a work bowl. *Note: the pieces of lemon grass are meant to be retained, even though they are inedible. This is important so that they can perfume the chicken. The experienced or prewarned diner will know to avoid them when eating.*

3. Add fish sauce, lime juice, roasted chilies *(page 40)* and the optional spicy rice to the chicken and mix well. Now, add green onion, chopped coriander and mint, and thinly sliced red pepper and red onion. Mix well, so that everything is integrated.

4. Line a serving dish with lettuce leaves and transfer chicken salad on top of it. Decorate with coriander and mint leaves and red pepper strips. Garnish the sides with lime wedges and slices of cucumber and tomato. This salad can be served immediately or it can wait for up to 1½ hour, unrefrigerated and lightly covered.

PORK

Phad Prik Moo
(Pork with Red Chili Sauce)

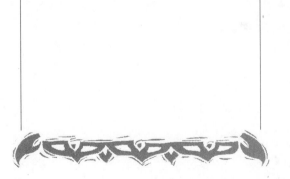

10 oz	trimmed pork tenderloin	300 g
½	medium green pepper	½
6	long green beans	6
5 tbsp	vegetable oil	70 mL
1 tsp	chopped garlic	5 mL
2 tbsp	red curry paste	25 mL
1 cup	water	250 mL
2 tbsp	fish sauce	25 mL
1 tbsp	sugar	15 mL
1 cup	bamboo shoot strips	250 mL
20	whole fresh basil leaves	20

Strips of red pepper

2½ cups	freshly steamed rice	625 mL

Serves 4.

This is an easy-to-make recipe that is ideal as a winter's eve's "pep-me-up". Aromatic with basil, spiced with red curry paste and full of crunchy vegetables, it is pleasurable, interesting and nutritious.

1. Slice tenderloin into strips that are ¼ inch/5 mm thick, 2 inch/5 cm long and about 1 inch/2.5 cm wide. If you find it difficult to cut thinly through fresh meat, leave it in the freezer for 15-20 minutes to harden slightly, and then slice. Reserve.
2. Cut pepper into 1-inch/2.5-cm squares. Trim ends of long beans and then chop into 1-inch/2.5-cm pieces. Reserve peppers and beans together.
3. Heat oil in a wok (or large frying pan) until it is just about to smoke. Lower heat and add garlic and curry paste and stir-fry for 45 seconds. Immediately add water and raise heat to maximum. Stir-cook for 1 minute and add fish sauce and sugar. Stir-cook for 2 minutes, until the sauce is smooth and bubbling.
4. Add reserved pork and stir-cook for 2 minutes. Add reserved peppers and long beans, as well as the bamboo shoot strips, and stir-cook for 4-5 minutes, until everything appears to be cooked and the sauce has thickened somewhat. Add ¾ of the basil leaves and stir into the sauce. Take off the fire and transfer to a serving dish. Top with some red pepper strips and the rest of the basil leaves. Serve immediately, accompanied by steamed rice.

Moo Kratiam
(Thai Garlic Pork)

When Thai people go for a picnic, they leave the burgers and potato salad at home and pack this garlic-fried pork instead. It tastes wonderful at beach temperature, especially when accompanied by the right sauce and some marinated cucumber.

10 oz	trimmed pork tenderloin	300 g
1 tbsp	chopped garlic	15 mL
2 tbsp	soya sauce	25 mL
½ tsp	black pepper	2 mL
1 tsp	sugar	5 mL
5 tbsp	vegetable oil	70 mL

Lettuce leaves
Strips of red pepper
Fresh coriander leaves
Thai Sweet and Sour Sauce
Cucumber Salad

Serves 4.

1. Slice tenderloin into strips that are ¼ inch/5 mm thick, 2 inches/5 cm long and about 1 inch/2.5 cm wide. If you find it difficult to cut thinly through fresh meat, leave it in the freezer for 15-20 minutes to harden slightly, and then slice.

2. Put the pieces on a large plate and sprinkle garlic, soya sauce, black pepper and sugar on them as evenly as possible. Toss and turn the pieces so that these marinating ingredients are distributed all over. Let the pork marinate for 2-3 minutes (up to ½ hour).

3. Heat oil in a wok (or large frying pan) until it is just about to smoke. Add pork and spread it out on the oil to it let brown, without turning, for 2-3 minutes. Turn and fry other side, again for 2-3 minutes. Now, stir-fry for another minute or so to ensure that all the pieces are browned. The cooking is done when all the liquids have evaporated, leaving the frying oil clear and the pork (more or less) uniformly browned. Remove meat from the wok onto a plate, leaving as much of the oil behind as possible.

4. Line a serving plate with lettuce and transfer pork onto it. Decorate with red pepper strips and coriander leaves. Serve immediately or reserve covered, for up to 2-3 hours, to be served at room temperature. Accompany with Thai Sweet and Sour Sauce *(page 38)* and Cucumber Salad *(page 23)*.

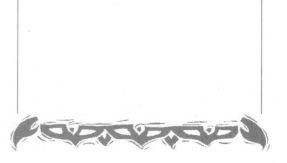

Moo Preow Waan
(Sweet and Sour Pork)

10 oz	trimmed pork tenderloin	300 g
½ tsp	tomato paste	2 mL
1 tbsp	water	15 mL
2 tbsp	fish sauce	25 mL
1 tbsp	rice (or white) vinegar	15 mL
1 tbsp	lime juice	15 mL
1 tbsp	sugar	15 mL
5 tbsp	vegetable oil	70 mL
1 tsp	chopped garlic	5 mL
¼	small onion, roughly chopped	¼
⅓	medium red pepper, in 1-inch/2.5-cm squares	⅓
½	small tomato, in 1-inch/2.5-cm chunks	½
1½ inches	English cucumber in 1-inch/2.5-cm wedges	3.5 cm
1 cup	pineapple in ½-inch/1-cm pieces	250 mL
1 tbsp	soya sauce	15 mL
¼ tsp	black pepper	1 mL
½ tsp	cornstarch	2 mL
1 tbsp	water	15 mL

For occasions that require a cheerful, colourful dish that is sweet rather than hot, Wandee concocted this multi-ingredient summer stew that will please both young and old. It'll especially please the cook, because, once all the ingredients have been prepped and organized, it takes all of 6 to 7 minutes to cook, even though it is complex, combining meat with fragile things like cucumber and pineapple.

1. Slice tenderloin into strips that are ¼ inch/5 mm thick, 2 inches/5 cm long and about 1 inch wide. If you find it difficult to cut thinly through fresh meat, leave it in the freezer for 15-20 minutes to harden slightly, and then slice. Reserve.
2. In a small bowl mix together tomato paste, water, fish sauce, vinegar, lime juice and sugar and beat until blended. Reserve.
3. Heat oil in a wok (or large frying pan) until it is just about to smoke. Add garlic and stir-fry for 30 seconds. Immediately add reserved pork and stir-fry for 2-3 minutes until all the pork has fried in the oil and is turning white. Add onion, red pepper, tomato, cucumber and pineapple as well as soya sauce and black pepper and stir-fry for 2 minutes, until all the vegetables have begun to wilt.
4. Add reserved sauce (tomato paste, etc.) from step #2. Stir-fry for 1-2 minutes until everything is integrated and shiny. Dissolve cornstarch in water, add to wok and stir-fry for less than a minute, until the sauce has thickened somewhat. Take off fire.

THE YOUNG THAILAND COOKBOOK

5. Transfer to a serving dish and sprinkle with black pepper. Top with strips of red pepper and coriander leaves. Serve immediately, accompanied by steamed rice.

Pinch black pepper
Strips of red pepper
Fresh coriander leaves

| 2½ cups | freshly | 625 mL |
| | steamed rice | |

Serves 4.

Fish and Seafood

Kaeng Khaiw Waan Pla (Fish With Hot Coconut Curry and Eggplant)

10 oz	kingfish (or grouper) filet, trimmed, deboned, skinned	300 g
1	Asian eggplant (5 oz/150 g)	1
2 cups	unsweetened coconut milk	500 mL
2 tbsp	green curry paste	25 mL
2	lime leaves, torn in thirds	2
2 tbsp	fish sauce	25 mL
1 tsp	sugar	5 mL
1/2	green pepper, in thin 1/4-inch/5-mm strips	1/2
1/2 cup	bamboo shoot strips	125 mL
1 cup	water	250 mL
20	whole fresh basil leaves	20
1 tbsp	green peas (frozen)	15 mL

A true Southern fishing village stew, this fiery, juicy dish offers solid nourishment and taste to spare. Its prime attraction is the coconut-milk rich sauce, flavoured with the citrous perfume of lime leaf and the sweet scent of basil. Its punch, which comes from the green chilies of the curry paste, underscores its main ingredients, the fish and the eggplant. Its ease of execution and failproof method are merely a bonus.

1. Cut fish into 1/2-inch/1-cm square chunks. Reserve.
2. Slice the eggplant into quarters lengthwise. Cut each quarter into 1/2-inch/1-cm pieces. Reserve.
3. Heat 1 cup/250 mL of the coconut milk in a wok (or large frying pan) on high heat, until it boils. Add green curry paste and, reducing the heat to medium, stir to dissolve in the coconut milk. Cook for 3 minutes until the oil of the coconut rises to the top. Add the second cup of coconut milk, the lime leaf, fish sauce and sugar and stir to mix. Immediately add the reserved fish and stir very gently to fold in. Increase heat to maximum, and let cook undisturbed for 2-3 minutes, until it's all bubbling happily and the fish is turning white.
4. Add eggplant, green pepper, bamboo shoots and 1 cup/250 mL water. Fold in gently and let cook for 2 minutes. Now stir (even more gently than before because the fish is cooked

Strips of red pepper

2½ cups	freshly	625 mL
	steamed rice	

Serves 4.

and will crumble very easily) folding vegetables to the bottom. Cook for 3-4 minutes undisturbed, until the eggplant is soft and the oil of the coconut has risen to the top.

5. Add ¾ of the basil leaves and the green peas. Fold in gently, and cook a final minute. Take off fire and transfer to a deep serving dish. Top with the rest of the basil and some red pepper strips. Serve immediately, accompanied by steamed rice.

A Feast of Fish

The next four recipes share one very important (and for Thai recipes, unusual) feature: all of them require that a piece of fish be grilled or fried and then topped with a sauce (instead of cooking the fish and the sauce together). It is possible, therefore, to use these four recipes for a "mix-and-match" fish-eating party, simply by presenting the fish on its own and four sauces on the side, to let the guests make up their own combinations.

Alternatively, it is possible to follow each recipe on its own and bring the fish already dressed to the table. If the more elaborate plan of multiple sauces is your choice (as it has been mine for several very successful dinner parties), then it is a good idea to present final enhancements like coriander or basil leaves and red pepper strips on a side plate, so that the guests can use them to garnish their own portions, after they have dressed their fish to their liking.

At YOUNG THAILAND, *Wandee uses fresh red snapper for both frying and grilling purposes. These head-on, rather expensive fish, which are hard to find fresh unless one is buying in bulk for a restaurant, are tricky for home-cooks. I recommend the easier-to-find and relatively foolproof grouper and salmon for frying and grilling, respectively.*

Pan-Fried Fish

1. Rub salt on both sides of the fish. Heat oil in a wok (or large frying pan) on high heat until it is just about to smoke. Add fish and fry for about 4 minutes each side, until cooked through and a little crispy on the edges. Remove from oil and serve as soon as possible.

1 lb	skin-on, boneless filet of grouper	500 g
¼ tsp	salt	1 mL
½ cup	vegetable oil	125 mL

Serves 4.

Grilled Fish

1. Combine salt, garlic and oil in a small bowl and mix to blend. Rub this mixture on both sides of the fish. Grill (or broil) fish for 3 minutes each side, until it is almost cooked through: with salmon it is desirable to leave about ¼ inch/ 5 mm in the centre underdone. The extra moisture of that pink heart adds to the texture immeasurably. If, however, underdone fish offends, then grill it 4-5 minutes each side for well done. Serve as soon as possible.

1 lb	skin-on, boneless filet of salmon	500 g
¼ tsp	salt	1 mL
1 tsp	chopped garlic	5 mL
1 tbsp	vegetable oil	15 mL

Serves 4.

Pla Krapong Paw (Grilled/Fried Fish with Coriander-Chili Sauce)

¼	medium red pepper, finely chopped	¼
¼	medium onion, finely chopped	¼
1 tbsp	finely chopped fresh coriander	15 mL
1 tsp	sugar	5 mL
1 tsp	chili-garlic sauce	5 mL
2 tbsp	lemon juice	25 mL
3 tbsp	soya sauce	45 mL
1 tbsp	vegetable oil	15 mL
1 lb	skin-on, boneless filet of salmon or grouper	500 g
	Wedges of lemon	
	Fresh coriander leaves	
2½ cups	freshly steamed rice	625 mL

Serves 4

This extremely simple sauce requires no cooking and can be made in advance. Akin to a Mexican salsa, it perks up the appetite in wondrous ways.

1. In a small bowl combine chopped red pepper, onion and coriander with sugar, chili-garlic sauce, lemon juice, soya sauce and oil. Beat a little to blend. Reserve.
2. Grill the salmon or fry the grouper *(page 113)*. Transfer to a serving plate and dress with several tablespoons of the reserved sauce. Stick wedges of lemon on the sides and top with coriander leaves. Serve immediately with the remainder of the sauce in a side bowl and accompanied by steamed rice.

Pla Preow Waan (Grilled/Fried Fish with Sweet and Sour Sauce)

Colourful and perky, this mild and complex sauce never fails to impress with its pleasant textures and tastes. It is best to make this one as required and serve it without reheating, in order to retain the integrity of its fragile ingredients. If you must reheat, then do it gently and far short of the boiling point.

1. In a work bowl combine tomato paste, 1 tbsp/15 mL water, vinegar, lemon juice, sugar and fish sauce. Mix well to blend. Reserve.

2. Heat oil in a wok (or frying pan) on high heat until it is just about to smoke. Add garlic and stir-fry for 30 seconds. Immediately add reserved sauce from step #1, and stir-cook for 1 minute. Add onion, red pepper, tomato, cucumber and pineapple and stir-fry for 1 minute. Add 2 tbsps/25 mL water and stir-fry for 1 minute, until it's bubbling happily. Dissolve cornstarch in 1 tbsp/15 mL of water, add to wok and stir-fry for 1 more minute, until the sauce has thickened somewhat. Take off fire and transfer to a bowl. Reserve covered to keep warm.

3. Grill the salmon or fry the grouper *(page 113)*. Transfer to a serving plate and smother with the reserved, warm sauce. Top with fresh coriander leaves and serve immediately, accompanied by steamed rice.

1/2 tsp	tomato paste	2 mL
1 tbsp	water	15 mL
2 tbsp	rice (or white) vinegar	25 mL
2 tbsp	lemon juice	25 mL
2 tbsp	sugar	25 mL
2 tbsp	fish sauce	25 mL
3 tbsp	vegetable oil	45 mL
1 tsp	chopped garlic	5 mL
1/2	small onion, roughly chopped	1/2
1/4	medium red pepper, in 1/2-inch/1-cm squares	1/4
1/2	small tomato, in 1/2-inch/1-cm pieces	1/2
1 inch	English cucumber, in 1/2-inch/1-cm wedges	2.5 cm
1 cup	pineapple, in 1/2-inch/1-cm pieces	250 mL
2 tbsp	water	25 mL
1/2 tsp	cornstarch	2 mL
1 tbsp	water	15 mL
1 lb	skin-on, boneless filet of salmon or grouper	500 g
	Fresh coriander leaves	
2 1/2 cups	freshly steamed rice	625 mL

Serves 4.

Pla Thod Sam Rod (Grilled/Fried Fish with Ginger-Tamarind Sauce)

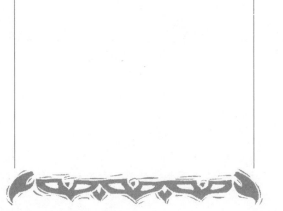

¼ cup	tamarind paste	50 mL
5 tbsp	warm water	70 mL
1 tbsp	soya sauce	15 mL
1 tbsp	fish sauce	15 mL
2 tbsp	sugar	25 mL
1 inch	ginger root	2.5 cm
3 tbsp	vegetable oil	45 mL
1 tsp	chopped garlic	5 mL
1	stem green onion, in 1-inch/2.5-cm pieces	1
¼	medium red pepper, in thin strips	¼
1 lb	skin-on, boneless filet of salmon or grouper	500 g

This mild, aromatic sauce is a perfect foil for the fleshiness of both salmon and grouper, while complementing other flavour combinations that might be served alongside it. It can be prepared in advance, kept covered and quickly reheated at the end, though not to boiling.

1. Combine tamarind paste with 5 tbsp/70 mL warm water in a small bowl and let soak for at least 15 minutes. Then mash it and transfer the mud-like mixture to a strainer set into a bowl. Mash and push with a spoon, forcing liquid to strain into the bowl. Scrape off the juice that clings to the underside of the strainer. You will have about 6 tbsp/90 mL of tamarind juice. (Discard the solids left in the strainer). To the tamarind juice in the bowl add soya sauce, fish sauce and sugar. Mix well to blend and reserve.

2. Peel the ginger root and cut into ⅛-inch/2.5-mm thick rounds. Stack a few rounds at a time and chop thinly to make shreds. Repeat until all the ginger has been shredded. Place the shreds in a strainer and run them under cold water. Drain and reserve.

3. Heat oil in a wok (or frying pan) on high heat until it is just about to smoke. Add garlic and stir-fry for 30 seconds. Immediately add reserved tamarind juice/soya sauce/fish sauce/sugar mixture and stir-cook for 1 minute. Add reserved ginger shreds, green onion pieces and half the red pepper strips.

Stir-fry for 1 minute. Take off fire and transfer to a bowl. Reserve covered to keep warm if to be used soon.

4. Grill the salmon or fry the grouper *(page 113)*. Transfer to a serving plate and smother with the reserved, warm sauce. Top with the remainder of the red pepper strips and plenty of fresh coriander leaves. Serve immediately, accompanied by steamed rice.

Fresh coriander leaves
2½ cups   freshly   625 mL
steamed rice

Serves 4.

Pla Tod
(Grilled/Fried Fish with Chili-Mushroom Sauce)

2 cups	unsweetened coconut milk	500 mL
2 tbsp	red curry paste	25 mL
1 tbsp	fish sauce	15 mL
2	lime leaves, torn into thirds	2
1 tbsp	sugar	15 mL
5 oz	mushrooms, thinly sliced	150 g
1 lb	skin-on, boneless, filet of salmon or grouper	500 g
	Fresh basil leaves	
	Strips of red pepper	
2½ cups	freshly steamed rice	625 mL

Serves 4.

The most assertive of this quartet of "fish with sauce" recipes, this sensual, creamy, spicy gravy, redolent of mushrooms and sweet-smooth coconut milk, is as user-friendly as it is magnificent. Ready in minutes, it can be successfully reheated or served lukewarm: excellent both ways. It's sunset velvet texture warms the eye, and its barrage of flavours gladdens the heart. Excellent as a cure for mid-winter blues.

1. Heat 1 cup/250 mL of the coconut milk in a wok (or frying pan) on high heat for 2 minutes until bubbling. Add red curry paste and stir to dissolve. Lower heat to medium-high and cook for 3 minutes until it has thickened and the oil of the coconut milk has risen to the top.

2. Add fish sauce, lime leaves and sugar. Stir-cook for 1 minute. Add second cup of coconut milk and all the mushrooms. Stir to blend. Raise heat to maximum and cook, stirring occasionally for 4-5 minutes until the oil of the coconut milk has returned to the top. Take off heat, and transfer to a bowl. Reserve covered to keep warm.

3. Grill the salmon or fry the grouper *(page 113)*. Transfer to a serving plate and smother with the reserved, warm sauce. Top with fresh basil leaves and red pepper strips. Serve immediately, accompanied by steamed rice.

Phad Kraphao Goong (Shrimps with Chili and Basil)

Simplicity and speed, hallmarks of Thai cuisine, really hit their stride in its seaside offerings. Thai seafood cookery works on the principle that the creatures of the deep, especially shrimps and squid, are so wonderful that one needs to do very little to them to enjoy them. Being Thai, however, means that nothing is left entirely to chance; the whole array of their amazing condiments turns what's already wonderful into sheer delicacy. This first recipe combines shrimps and a traditionally flavoured sauce with crunchy peppers and the perfume of sweet basil.

1. Heat oil in a wok (or large frying pan) on high heat until it is just about to smoke. Add garlic and hot chilies simultaneously, and stir-fry for 30 seconds. Add shrimps and peppers, stir-frying for 30 seconds. Add soya sauce, fish sauce and sugar and stir-fry for 30 more seconds.
2. Add water and oyster sauce and stir-fry for 1 minute. Add ¾ of the basil leaves and stir in. Dissolve cornstarch in water, add to wok and stir-fry for a final 30 seconds until the sauce has thickened somewhat, and the shrimps are glistening and plumply pink-white. Take off fire.
3. Transfer to a serving dish and top with the remainder of the basil and some thin strips of red pepper. Serve immediately, accompanied by steamed rice.

5 tbsp	vegetable oil	70 mL
1 tsp	chopped garlic	5 mL
4	fresh hot chilies, finely chopped	4
16	large shrimps, shelled and deveined (10 oz/300 g)	16
½	medium red pepper, in 1-inch/2.5-cm squares	½
½	medium green pepper, in 1-inch/2.5-cm squares	½
2 tbsp	soya sauce	25 mL
1 tbsp	fish sauce	15 mL
1 tsp	sugar	5 mL
4 tbsp	water	50 mL
1 tsp	oyster sauce	5 mL
20	whole leaves fresh basil	20
½ tsp	cornstarch	2 mL
1 tbsp	water	15 mL
	Strips of red pepper	
2½ cups	freshly steamed rice	625 mL

Serves 2-4.

Goong Kratiam
(Garlic Shrimps)

16	large shrimps, shelled and deveined (10 oz/300 g)	16
1 tbsp	sugar	15 mL
2 tbsp	soya sauce	25 mL
1 tsp	oyster sauce	5 mL
1 tsp	black pepper	5 mL
1 tbsp	chopped garlic	15 mL
5 tbsp	vegetable oil	70 mL

Lettuce leaves
Strips of red pepper
Fresh coriander leaves
Slices of tomato and cucumber
Thai Lemon-Coriander Sauce

*Serves 4 as an appetizer
or 2 as a main course
with steamed rice.*

This is the house favourite at Young Thailand, *outsold only by* Pad Thai *and Spring Rolls. Still, being a close third to those leviathans is no mean accomplishment, and after a single taste of these sweet and mysterious shrimps, you'll know why. Not only that, but they're ready in 3 minutes and are equally enjoyable hot or at room temperature; ideal for the buffet and for picnics, as well as for an intimate supper.*

1. In a work bowl combine shrimps, sugar, soya sauce, oyster sauce, black pepper and garlic. Toss and mix so that all the shrimps are thoroughly coated in these marinating ingredients. Let sit for 3-5 minutes, uncovered and unrefrigerated.

2. Heat oil in a wok (or large frying pan) on high heat until it is just about to smoke. Add the shrimps and their marinade and stir-fry on maximum heat for 3 minutes, allowing all the shrimps to be seared in the hot oil, browned and plump. Take off fire.

3. Line a serving plate with lettuce leaves and transfer the shrimps onto the lettuce. Top with red pepper strips and fresh coriander leaves and garnish with slices of tomato and cucumber. These shrimps can be served immediately or they can wait, lightly covered and unrefrigerated for up to 2 hours. Accompany them with Thai Lemon-Coriander Sauce *(page 39)*.

Goong Tod
(Marinated Fried Shrimps)

Pleasantly spiced and lightly dredged in flour, these relatively grease-less fried shrimps can be prepared in advance and finished in a snap when ready to serve. They even work if pre-fried and offered at room temperature. Ideal for a party buffet or a lazy, al fresco lunch by the shade of a tree (be it palm or maple).

1. In a work bowl combine soya sauce, garlic and sugar. Add shrimp and mix well to coat thoroughly. Proceed immediately, or cover and refrigerate the shrimps for up to 2 hours.
2. In a separate bowl, combine flour, black pepper and salt, stirring to mix thoroughly.
3. Transfer the shrimps into the flour bowl. Toss to coat shrimps thoroughly. Transfer the dredged shrimps into a strainer. Hold the strainer over a sink and shake to allow excess flour to sieve through.
4. Heat oil in a wok (or large frying pan) on high heat, until it is just about to smoke. Add the dredged shrimp and stir-fry for a maximum of 3 minutes, allowing all of them to fry evenly in the oil. They are done when they have become golden brown with pink highlights. Remove them from the oil immediately with a slotted spoon and lay them out on a plate to shed their excess oil. The oil left in the wok can be discarded.
5. Line a serving plate with lettuce leaves and transfer the fried shrimps onto it. Top with red pepper strips and coriander leaves. Stick a couple of lemon wedges on the sides and serve (immediately or later) accompanied by bowls of Thai Sweet and Sour Sauce *(page 38)* and YOUNG THAILAND Hot Sauce *(page 37)*.

16	large shrimps, shelled and deveined (10 oz/300 g)	16
1 tbsp	soya sauce	15 mL
1 tbsp	chopped garlic	15 mL
½ tsp	sugar	2 mL
½ cup	flour	125 mL
1 tbsp	black pepper	15 mL
½ tsp	salt	2 mL
1 cup	vegetable oil	250 mL

Lettuce leaves
Strips of red pepper
Fresh coriander leaves
Wedges of lemon
Thai Sweet and Sour Sauce
YOUNG THAILAND Hot Sauce

Serves 4 as an appetizer or 2 as a main course with steamed or fried rice.

Goong Ma Kam (Shrimps Braised in Tamarind Sauce)

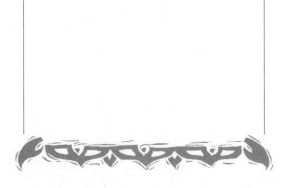

¼ cup	tamarind paste	50 mL
¼ cup	warm water	50 mL
1 inch	ginger root	2.5 cm
5 tbsp	vegetable oil	70 mL
1 tsp	chopped garlic	5 mL
5 tbsp	water	70 mL
1 tbsp	sugar	15 mL
1 tsp	fish sauce	15 mL
1 tbsp	soya sauce	15 mL
16	large shrimps, shelled and deveined (10 oz/300 g)	16
1	stem green onion, in 1-inch/2.5-cm pieces	1
¼	medium red pepper in thin strips	¼

This is a mild, sweet and sour shrimp recipe, that, as always, leaves the shrimps springy and vibrant with a sauce that leaves the mouth yearning for more. It is cooked at lightning speed yet ends up with a complex, delicately scented sauce. A very valuable recipe for company that shirks from spice, while demanding interesting flavours.

1. Combine tamarind paste with ¼ cup/50 mL warm water in a small bowl and let soak for at least 15 minutes. Then mash it and transfer the mud-like mixture to a strainer set into a bowl. Mash and push with a spoon, forcing liquid to strain into the bowl. Scrape off the juice that clings to the underside of the strainer. You will have about 5 tbsp/70 mL of tamarind juice. Reserve it. Discard the solids left in the strainer.

2. Peel the ginger root and cut into ⅛-inch/2.5 mm thick rounds. Stack a few rounds at a time and chop thinly to make shreds. Repeat until all the ginger has been shredded. Place the shreds in a strainer and run them under cold water. Drain and reserve.

3. Heat oil in a wok (or large frying pan) on high heat, until it is just about to smoke. Add garlic and stir-fry for 30 seconds. Lower heat to medium and immediately add reserved tamarind juice. Stir-cook for 30 seconds. Add water, sugar, fish sauce and soya sauce. Raise heat to maximum and cook, stirring for 1 minute.

Fresh coriander leaves

2½ cups · · · · · freshly · · · · · 625 mL
steamed rice

4. Add reserved ginger shreds and stir-cook for 1 minute. Add shrimps and stir-cook for 2 minutes, until they are springy and pink-white. Take off fire.

5. Transfer to a serving dish and top with green onion pieces, red pepper strips, and fresh coriander leaves. Serve immediately, accompanied by steamed rice.

Serves 2-4.

Tod Mun Goong
(Thai Shrimp-Cakes)

40	medium shrimps	40
	(12 oz/375 g)	
1 tbsp	red curry paste	15 mL
1	egg yolk	1
6	long green beans	6
3	lime leaves	3
1 cup	vegetable oil	250 mL

Lettuce leaves
Strips of red pepper
Fresh coriander leaves
Slices of orange
Cucumber Salad

1 tbsp	roasted unsalted	15 mL
	peanuts ground to a	
	coarse meal	

Thai Sweet and Sour Sauce

*Serves 6-8 as an appetizer
or 4 as a main course with
steamed or fried rice.*

Much as Wandee and I are making a point of avoiding the deep-fried specialties of Thai cuisine, some items are just too good to resist. This delicate, tender and crunchy all at once, spicy and sweet shrimp-cake is definitely something for which to overlook both the calories and the inconvenience of frying. Textured with finely chopped green beans and deeply flavoured with red curry paste as well as lime leaf, these delicious morsels satisfy as wonderfully on a party buffet, or at a picnic, as they do as a cosy dinner's main course.

1. Thoroughly chop-mince the shrimps (by hand or by processor) to a pulp. Transfer to a work bowl and add red curry paste. Mix to blend thoroughly. Add egg yolk and stir in. Trim and then finely (1/8 inch/2.5 mm) chop the green beans. Add to the shrimps and stir in. Shred the lime leaves very finely (thread-like) and add to the shrimps. Now give everything one good mixing, until integrated. You can proceed with the recipe, or, at this point, you can cover and refrigerate the shrimp mixture for up to 3 hours.

2. Heat oil in a wok (or large frying pan) on high heat until it is just about to smoke. Turn down heat to medium and add shrimp-cakes thus: take a tablespoonful at a time and, using a second tablespoon, flatten it out somewhat and then slide it off the first spoon into the oil. Repeat as fast as possible with another seven such dollops which will fit comfortably in the oil. Fry the cakes for 2 minutes on one side, and then carefully turn them over: they'll have turned golden, with some charred edges. Fry the second side for 2 minutes and then

turn them yet again for 30-40 seconds each side, to give them the perfect golden browning. Remove them from the oil onto a plate, without stacking them, so that they can shed excess oil. Repeat the frying procedure with the remainder of your shrimp mixture, which should give you another 8 cakes, for a total of 16.

3. Line a serving plate with lettuce leaves and transfer the shrimp-cakes onto it. Top the cakes with red pepper strips and coriander leaves and arrange orange slices along the edges. Serve immediately (or later, to be enjoyed lukewarm), accompanied by Cucumber Salad *(page 23)* on which you have sprinkled ground peanuts, and also a side bowl of Thai Sweet and Sour Sauce *(page 38)*.

It is important to fry these cakes without burning them. If yours are turning too dark, it means either that they're over-done or that your heat is on too high. The frying oil left in the wok at the end of the frying can be discarded.

Another popular version of this recipe uses minced fish instead of shrimps. Just replace the shrimps with 1 lb/500 g of fish filets.

2 oz	glass noodles (bean threads)	60 g
16	large shrimps, shelled and deveined (10 oz/300 g)	16
1/2	lemon	1/2
1	stem lemon grass	1
	Handful whole fresh coriander leaves	
20	whole basil leaves	20
1 tsp	chopped garlic	5 mL
1/2 tsp	black pepper	2 mL
2 tbsp	soya sauce	25 mL
4 tbsp	white (or rice) wine	50 mL
1/4	medium red pepper, in thin strips	1/4
1 1/2 oz	salted butter	45 g
1/2 cup	water	125 mL

Additional coriander leaves,
basil leaves and
strips of red pepper
Wedges of lemon

*Serves 2 as a main course
or 4 as a noodle course.*

Goong Oap
(Butter-Steamed Shrimps with Glass Noodles)

Here is an oasis, safe from the dizzying heat and spice, a plateful of pink-white shrimps in a benevolent sauce of butter and lemon, mantled in a cloud of glass noodles. Easy to concoct as an additional dish at a dinner party, it'll prove the sleeper hit of the meal, with its subtle taste and pastel, summery colours.

1. Soak glass noodles in plenty of cold water for about 1 hour. Transfer to a strainer to drain out excess water. The noodles will have swollen to 3 times their original volume. Transfer them to a work bowl.

2. Add shrimps to the noodles and squeeze lemon juice onto the shrimps, adding lemon rind as well.

3. Smash lemon grass with the flat of a chef's knife once and chop into 1-inch/2.5-cm pieces. Add to the shrimps. Add coriander leaves and basil leaves.

4. In a separate bowl combine garlic, black pepper, soya sauce and wine. Sprinkle this mixture evenly over the shrimps. Add red pepper strips and fold in the ingredients once or twice. This may be kept for up to 2 hours, refrigerated and covered, until ready to cook.

5. Heat a soup pot on high heat to get it red hot (about 2 minutes). Add the chunk of butter, then immediately add the reserved mixture of shrimps and noodles, with all the marinating liquids. Cover the pot and cook for 2 minutes. During this cooking, shake the pot a couple of times to mix things up, but do not uncover.

6. Uncover, stir the contents and push down any noodles that might have cooked onto the sides of the pot. Add ½ cup/ 125 mL water and cover again. Cook for 3 more minutes, shaking the pot a couple of times during this cooking. Uncover and stir. The shrimps will be pink-white, the noodles transparent and soft and most of the sauce absorbed. Take off fire.

7. Transfer to a serving dish. Top with the additional red pepper strips, coriander and basil leaves and stick a couple of lemon wedges on the side. Serve immediately.

Apologize to guests for the presence of the inedible lemon rind and lemon grass bits that end up in this dish. It is traditional to serve them, to prolong their flavour in the dish.

Goong Preow Waan
(Sweet and Sour Shrimps)

4 tbsp	vegetable oil	50 mL
1 tsp	chopped garlic	5 mL
16	large shrimps, shelled and deveined (10 oz/300 g)	16
½	small onion, roughly chopped	½
½	medium green pepper, in ½-inch/1-cm squares	½
½	small tomato, in ½-inch/1-cm pieces	½
1½ inch	cucumber, in ½-inch/1-cm wedges	3.5 cm
1 cup	pineapple, in ½-inch/1-cm pieces	250 mL
2 tbsp	fish sauce	25 mL
½ tsp	tomato paste	2 mL
7 tbsp	water	95 mL
1 tbsp	sugar	15 mL
3 tbsp	rice (or white) vinegar	45 mL
1	stem green onion, in 1-inch/2.5-cm pieces	1
½ tsp	cornstarch	2 mL
1 tbsp	water	15 mL

Pinch of black pepper
Strips of red pepper
Fresh coriander leaves

2½ cups	freshly steamed rice	625 mL

Serves 3-4.

A lively sauce can tend to overwhelm fragile morsels like shrimps, unless one strikes an exact balance between salt, sour and sweet. Wandee's formula strives for harmony and achieves it with gusto.

1. Heat oil in a wok (or large frying pan) on high heat until it is just about to smoke. Add garlic and stir-fry for 10 seconds (two stirs). Immediately add shrimps and stir them in a couple of times (10 seconds). Add onion, green pepper, tomato, cucumber, pineapple and fish sauce, and fold everything in. Turn down heat to medium and let cook for 1-2 minutes, until the shrimps begin to turn pink-white.
2. In a small work bowl combine tomato paste, water, sugar and vinegar. Mix well to blend. Add to the wok and turn up heat to maximum. Stir-fry for 1 minute. Add green onion and cornstarch dissolved in water. Stir-fry for 1 more minute until the sauce has thickened somewhat and everything is bubbling happily. Take off heat.
3. Transfer to a deep serving dish and sprinkle black pepper. Top with red pepper strips and coriander leaves and serve immediately, accompanied by steamed rice.

Chu Chi Goong (Shrimps in Spicy Coconut Milk)

In a way, this easy-to-make coconut milk-red curry paste-lime leaf sauce is the taste and flavour combination that defines Thai cooking more than any other. Here it constitutes the only adornment for undercooked shrimps in an elegant combination whose every last mouthful is pleasure itself.

1. Slice the lime leaves as thinly as possible (thread-like is best). Reserve.
2. Heat 1 cup/250 mL of the coconut milk in a wok (or large frying pan) on high heat until it comes to a boil. Turn heat down to medium and add red curry paste and stir to dissolve, cooking for 1–2 minutes until the oil of the coconut milk rises to the surface. Add sugar and ½ of the reserved lime leaf shreds. Stir-fry for 30 seconds. Add fish sauce and second cup of coconut milk. Turn heat up to maximum and stir-cook for 1 minute. Add shrimps and fold into the sauce. Cook for 2–3 minutes, stirring occasionally, until the shrimps have turned pink-white and springy and the oil of the coconut milk has once again risen to the surface. Take off fire.
3. Transfer to a serving dish and top with the rest of the lime leaf shreds, basil leaves and strips of red pepper. Serve immediately, accompanied by steamed rice.

2	lime leaves	2
2 cups	unsweetened coconut milk	500 mL
2 tbsp	red curry paste	25 mL
1 tbsp	sugar	15 mL
1 tsp	fish sauce	15 mL
16	large shrimps, shelled and deveined (10 oz/300 g)	16
	Basil leaves	
	Strips of red pepper	
2½ cups	freshly steamed rice	625 mL

Serves 2-4.

Phad Phrik Khing Goong (Shrimps with Green Beans in Chili Sauce)

4 tbsp	vegetable oil	50 mL
2 tbsp	red curry paste	25 mL
2	lime leaves in quarters	2
1 cup	water	250 mL
16	large shrimps, shelled and deveined (10 oz/300 g)	16
14	long green beans, trimmed and cut in 1-inch/2.5-cm pieces	14
1 tbsp	sugar	15 mL

Strips of red pepper
Fresh coriander leaves

2½ cups	freshly steamed rice	625 mL

Serves 3-4.

The distinguishing feature and the particular attraction of this dish is its pretty combination of green with pink, of crisp green beans with springy shrimps, in a darkly delicious, easy-to-achieve curry sauce. It tends to appear slightly oilier than the coconut milk-based curries because there is no coconut milk used to bind it. It is, however, not all that rich, though it tastes as if it were, and enhances steamed rice most wonderfully.

1. Heat oil in a wok (or large frying pan) on high heat until it is just about to smoke. Add red curry paste and stir to dissolve for 30 seconds. Turn heat down to medium-low and stir-cook for another 30 seconds. Add lime leaf and stir-fry for 1 minute. Turn heat back to maximum and add ½ cup/ 125 mL of the water and stir-cook for 1 minute.
2. Add shrimps, green beans and sugar. Stir-fry for 1 minute. Turn heat down to medium high, and add the rest of the water (½ cup/125 mL). Cook for 2-3 minutes, stirring occasionally, until shrimps are pink-white and springy. Take off heat.
3. Transfer to a serving dish and top with red pepper strips and coriander leaves. Serve immediately with steamed rice.

Blamuek Phad Prik
(Squid in Spicy Sauce)

The inexpensive but delicious squid is redefined in this easy and colourful recipe that leaves it tender and crispy, bathed in a robustly spiced sauce. The dish is balanced with vegetables and perfumed sweetly with fresh basil.

1. Heat oil in a wok (or large frying pan) on high heat until it is just about to smoke. Add red curry paste and the lime leaves and stir to dissolve. Turn heat down to medium and add water. Stir-cook for 2 minutes until the sauce is bubbling happily and releasing its flavours.

2. Add fish sauce, soya sauce and sugar and stir-cook for 30 seconds. Add squid, bamboo shoots, pepper squares and green beans and stir to mix. Increase heat to maximum and stir-fry for 2-3 minutes until the squid has turned milk-white and textured and the vegetables are wilted and shiny.

3. Add ¾ of the basil leaves, stir and take off fire. Transfer to a serving dish and top with the rest of the basil and some thin strips of red pepper. Serve immediately, accompanied by steamed rice.

5 tbsp	vegetable oil	70 mL
2 tbsp	red curry paste	25 mL
2	lime leaves, torn into thirds	2
5 tbsp	water	70 mL
1 tbsp	fish sauce	15 mL
1 tbsp	soya sauce	15 mL
1 tsp	sugar	5 mL
8 oz	cleaned squid, cut in 1-inch/2.5-cm rounds	150 g
½ cup	bamboo shoot strips	125 mL
½	red (or green) pepper, in 1-inch/2.5-cm squares	½
5	long green beans, trimmed and cut in 1-inch/2.5-cm pieces	5
20	whole fresh basil leaves	20
	Strips of red pepper	
2½ cups	freshly steamed rice	625 mL

Serves 3-4.

Hoy Maeng Phou Oap (Steamed Mussels with Lemon Grass)

28	mussels	28
	(fresh and cleaned, or frozen)	
2 oz	salted butter	60 g
1	stem lemon grass	1
30	basil leaves	30
½ cup	fresh coriander leaves	125 mL
1 tbsp	chopped garlic	15 mL
1 tsp	black pepper	5 mL
½ cup	white (or rice) wine	125 mL
2	limes	2
2 tbsp	soya sauce	25 mL
½	medium red pepper, in thin strips	½

Additional fresh coriander leaves
YOUNG THAILAND Hot Sauce

*Serves 4 as an appetizer
or 2 as a main course with
steamed rice.*

Mussels steamed in an aromatic broth is a delicious practice of all maritime countries, with Thailand no exception. This recipe is as easy to make as the very popular moules marinières *of French cookery and makes for a pleasant, lemon-limey alternative to it.*

1. Place mussels in a work bowl. Add chunk of butter.
2. Smash lemon grass with the flat of a chef's knife once and chop into 1-inch/2.5-cm pieces. Add to the mussels.
3. Add basil leaves, coriander leaves, garlic, black pepper and wine. Stir a few times.
4. Cut limes into quarters. Squeeze the quarters directly onto the mussels and then add the rinds to the mussels. Sprinkle soya sauce evenly over all and stir a few more times. If you wish, you can make up the recipe to this point and keep for up to one hour. Simply cover and refrigerate the work bowl and proceed with the recipe when ready. Alternatively, proceed after a 2-3-minute wait, once all the above ingredients have been combined.
5. Place a large pot with a lid on high heat to get it red hot (about 2 minutes). Transfer the mussels and all the marinating ingredients into the pot, cover tightly and cook for 2 minutes. During this cooking, shake the pot a couple of times to mix things up, but do not uncover.

THE YOUNG THAILAND COOKBOOK

6. Still on high heat, uncover the pot and stir the mussels several times to bring the ones from the bottom up to the top. Add half of the red pepper strips and cook for 1 more minute, until it's all bubbling happily. Take off fire.
7. Transfer to a deep serving dish, along with all of its broth. Top with the remaining red pepper strips and some fresh coriander leaves. Serve immediately with a bowl of YOUNG THAILAND Hot Sauce (*page 37*) on the side.

Absolutely fresh mussels are an impossibility in areas that are far from the sea. Wandee uses frozen Kiwi mussels that arrive on the half-shell and ready to use. There is a slight loss of texture due to the freezing, but at least one is able to avoid the curse of the one bad mussel, which can always slip into an order of freshly imported mollusks and which can ruin one's appetite for mussels forever.

Phad Phed Talay
(Seafood with Eggplant and Chili)

5 tbsp	vegetable oil	70 mL
1 tsp	chopped garlic	5 mL
4	fresh hot chilies, finely chopped	4
1	Asian eggplant, sliced diagonally in 2-inch/5-cm chunks	1
4 oz	cleaned squid, cut in ½-inch/1-cm rings	125 g
8	large shrimps, shelled and deveined (5 oz/150 g)	8
4	crab claws (frozen)	4
5	long green beans, trimmed and cut in 1-inch/2.5-cm pieces	5
3 tbsp	soya sauce	45 mL
1 tbsp	fish sauce	15 mL
½	red (or green) pepper, in 1-inch/2.5-cm squares	½
½ cup	bamboo shoot strips	125 mL
5 tbsp	water	70 mL
1 tsp	sugar	5 mL
20	whole fresh basil leaves	20
½ tsp	cornstarch	2 mL
1 tbsp	water	15 mL

Strips of red pepper

2½ cups	freshly steamed rice	625 mL

Serves 4.

This lively stew showcases a trio of seafoods partnered with several vegetables in a delightfully simple sauce. Wandee ignores all the eggplant lore that intimidates with tales of salting and lengthy baking. She simply chops it up and throws it in the wok, to end up with a lovely texture and a fresh taste.

1. Heat oil in a wok (or large frying pan) on high heat until it is just about to smoke. Add garlic and hot chilies simultaneously and stir-fry for 10 seconds (two stirs). Add eggplant and stir-fry for 1 minute until all the pieces have touched the oil and have started to fry on all sides.

2. Add all the seafood (squid, shrimp and crab claws), as well as the green beans, and stir-fry for 30 seconds. Add soya sauce and fish sauce and stir-fry for 30 seconds. Add pepper squares and bamboo shoots and stir-fry for 30 seconds. Add water and sugar and cook, stirring often for 3 minutes.

3. Add ¾ of the basil leaves and stir them in. Dissolve cornstarch in water, add to wok and stir-fry for a final 30 seconds, until the sauce has thickened somewhat and everything is well tossed together and shiny. Take off fire.

4. Transfer to a serving dish and top with the remainder of the basil and some thin strips of red pepper. Serve immediately with steamed rice.

Pad Po Tak
(Mixed Seafood in Thai Green Curry)

Just like its cousin, the Kaeng Khiao Wan Kai *(Chicken in Thai Green Curry), this dish exhilarates with its extra hot, extra flavourful sauce and its tender morsels. Seafood and the occasional crunchy pepper in a truly irresistible sauce: eating does not get much better.*

Normally lemon grass is cut in big (1-inch/2.5-cm) pieces and can be easily avoided when eating, whereas this recipe calls for this hard-to-chew aromatic to be finely shredded and dispersed throughout the sauce, making it impossible to avoid. The fine shredding does make it a little easier to chew, but it's still sharp and hard and can be annoying to the uninitiated. If you prefer, cut the lemon grass into larger pieces, and use at the same time as the shreds are indicated below.

2 cups	unsweetened coconut milk	500mL
2 tbsp	green curry paste	25 mL
4 oz	grouper (or kingfish) filet, in 1/2-inch/1-cm chunks	125 g
2	lime leaves, cut into thirds	2
8	mussels (preferably Kiwi)	8
1 tsp	fish sauce	5 mL
1 tsp	sugar	5 mL
8	large shrimps, shelled and deveined (5 oz/150 g)	8
4 oz	cleaned squid, in 1-inch/2.5-cm rings	125 g
1	stem lemon grass, finely chopped (1/8-1/16 inch/2.5-1.25 mm)	1
1/2	medium red pepper, in 1-inch/2.5-cm squares	1/2
20	leaves fresh basil	20
	Strips of red pepper	
2 1/2 cups	freshly steamed rice	625 mL

Serves 4.

1. Heat 1 cup/250 mL of the coconut milk in a wok (or large frying pan) on high heat until it boils. Add green curry paste and stir to dissolve. Stir-cook for 1 minute.

2. Add grouper and the lime leaves and second cup of coconut milk. Cook, stirring for 1 minute. Add mussels, fish sauce and sugar and stir-cook for 1 minute. Add shrimps, squid and lemon grass and fold in. Cook, stirring gently for one minute.

3. Add red peppers and fold in. Cook for 30 seconds. Add 2/3 of the basil leaves and fold in gently. Cook for 1 minute. Take off heat.

4. Transfer to a deep serving dish and top with the red pepper strips and the rest of the basil leaves. Serve immediately with steamed rice.

Vegetables

Stir-Fried Mixed Vegetables

½	bunch broccoli	½
½	large carrot	½
4 oz	mushrooms	125 g
4 oz	baby corn (canned)	125 g
3 oz	snow peas	90 g
5 tbsp	vegetable oil	70 mL
1 tsp	chopped garlic	5 mL
1 cup	water	250 mL
3 tbsp	soya sauce	45 mL
1 tsp	sesame oil	5 mL
½ tsp	black pepper	2 mL
½ tsp	cornstarch	2 mL
1 tbsp	water	15 mL

Strips of red pepper
Fresh coriander leaves

*Serves 2 as a vegetarian main course
with steamed rice
or 4 as a vegetable course.*

This is the most well known and easiest to concoct of the Asian vegetable stir-fries. Wandee's version is subtly flavoured with sesame oil and uses absolutely no animal-derived ingredients. The choice of vegetables is flexible. Cauliflower can be used instead of broccoli; roughly chopped onion can be added; thinly sliced bamboo shoot can replace the baby corn; and so on. This same recipe can work with whatever odds and ends of vegetable are on hand, and to make it pretty, one simply needs to chop or slice them in thin and attractive morsels.

1. Cut off thick stem of the broccoli and reserve for another use. Separate the flowering part into individual florets. Transfer into a work bowl. Slice the carrot into thin (1/16-inch/1.25-mm) rounds. Add to the broccoli. Quarter the mushrooms and add to the work bowl. Wash and drain the baby corn and add to the work bowl. Remove the strings of the snow peas and add to the rest of the vegetables. Reserve all of these together.
2. Heat oil in a wok (or large frying pan) on high heat, until it is just about to smoke. Add garlic and stir-fry for 30 seconds. Add all the reserved vegetables at once and stir-fry for 30 seconds, until they have all touched the hot oil. Add water, and let it come to bubbling. Turn heat down to medium and cover the wok. Let it cook undisturbed for 1 minute.
3. Uncover and turn up heat. Stir-fry for 1 minute. Add soya sauce and stir-fry for 1 minute. Sprinkle sesame oil and black pepper evenly and stir in. Dissolve cornstarch in water, add to wok and stir-fry for 1 minute, until the sauce has thickened somewhat. Take off fire.
4. Transfer to a deep serving dish and top with red pepper strips and fresh coriander leaves. Serve immediately.

Pud Ka Na
(Green Vegetables with Oyster Sauce)

This recipe can be made with any of the many available Asian greens, the deciding factor being one of taste. You can choose the bitter (Chinese broccoli), the medium (bok-choy), or the sweet (snow-pea greens), to name but three.

1. Heat oil in a wok (or large frying pan) on high heat, until it is just about to smoke. Add garlic and stir-fry for 30 seconds. Add greens and water and stir-fry for 1-2 minutes, until the greens have started to wilt. Add oyster sauce and soya sauce. Stir-fry for 1 minute. Dissolve cornstarch in water, add to wok and stir-fry for 1 minute. Take off fire.
2. Transfer to a serving dish and top with red pepper strips and coriander leaves. Serve immediately.

5 tbsp	vegetable oil	70 mL
1 tsp	chopped garlic	5 mL
1	bunch (14 oz/425 g)	1

Asian greens, roughly chopped
in 2-inch/5-cm pieces

½ cup	water	125 mL
1 tbsp	oyster sauce	15 mL
1 tsp	soya sauce	5 mL
½ tsp	cornstarch	2 mL
1 tbsp	cold water	15 mL

Strips of red pepper
Fresh coriander leaves

Serves 4 as a vegetable course.

Vegetable and Tofu Curry

1/2	bunch broccoli	1/2
1/2	large carrot	1/2
4 oz	mushrooms	125 g
4 oz	baby corn (canned)	125 g
3 oz	snow peas	90 g
4 oz	fried tofu	125 g
2 cups	unsweetened coconut milk	500 mL
2 tbsp	red curry paste	25 mL
1/2 tsp	sugar	2 mL
1 cup	water	250 mL
1 tbsp	fish sauce	15 mL
1 tbsp	green peas (frozen)	15 mL
1/4	medium red pepper, in thin strips	1/4
20	whole fresh basil leaves	20
2 1/2 cups	freshly steamed rice	625 mL

Serves 2-3.

The fried tofu that is needed can be purchased already fried, or prepared at home by frying the tofu, 3 minutes each side, in 4 tbsp/50 mL vegetable oil.

This sunset-coloured, festive creation makes for a lovely vegetable-based meal, with the addition of rice and stir-fried greens. The vegetables of this recipe (as those of the Stir-Fried Mixed Vegetables) are a matter of choice, with replacements and additions as one sees fit.

1. Cut off thick stem of the broccoli and reserve for another use. Separate the flowering part into individual florets. Transfer into a work bowl. Slice the carrot into thin (1/16-inch/1.25-mm) rounds. Add to the broccoli. Quarter the mushrooms and add to the work bowl. Wash and drain the baby corn and add to the work bowl. Remove the strings of the snow peas and add to the rest of the vegetables. Reserve all these together.

2. Slice the fried tofu cake into three and cut crosswise into three to obtain nine 1/2-inch/1-cm cubes. Reserve.

3. Heat 1 cup/250 mL of the coconut milk in a wok (or large frying pan) on high heat until it boils. Add the red curry paste and the sugar and stir-cook for 1 minute to dissolve the additions and to allow the oil of the coconut milk to rise. Add all the reserved vegetables at once, as well as the second cup of the coconut milk and the water. Stir-cook for 1 minute so that all the vegetables are coated by the sauce.

4. Add reserved tofu and fish sauce. Fold into the vegetables gently and let cook for 2-3 minutes (folding just one time during this period), until the oil of the coconut milk has risen to the surface and everything is bubbling happily.

5. Add green peas, half the red pepper strips and 2/3 of the basil leaves. Fold in very gently to avoid breaking the tofu and cook for one minute. Take off fire and transfer to a deep serving dish. Top with the rest of the red pepper strips and the rest of the basil. Serve immediately with steamed rice.

Thai Spicy Eggplant

Eggplant is a vegetable one grows into. Its smooth texture and particular flavour, which blend so harmoniously with oil, garlic and herbs, are decidedly adult pleasures. This spicy Thai recipe, which combines fried eggplant with onion, garlic, basil and peppers works wonders on the palate, offering proof positive that growing up has its rewards.

The Asian variety of eggplant, with its lapis lazuli skin and its delicate, slender body, is more suitable because it cooks up more attractively than would the thicker, deeply purple Mediterranean kind.

1. Heat 1 cup oil/250 mL in a wok (or large frying pan) on high heat, until it is just about to smoke. Add eggplant and spread out in the oil. Fry for 2 minutes, then turn and fry the other side for 2 minutes. Continue flipping pieces over for another minute, until they are nicely browned and glistening and the flesh of the eggplant is soft and can be pierced easily. Remove the eggplant pieces from the oil with a slotted spoon and transfer to a strainer set over a bowl to drain off as much as possible of the excess oil. Discard the oil in the wok, wipe it clean and return it to the fire.

2. Add 2 tbsp/25mL oil to the wok and immediately add garlic and chilies and stir-fry for 30 seconds. Add onion and ⅔ of the red pepper strips and stir-fry for 10 seconds. Add the fried eggplant and stir in. Immediately add soya sauce, sugar and water and stir-fry for 1-2 minutes until everything is bubbling happily. Add ⅔ of the basil leaves and the cornstarch dissolved in water. Stir-fry for 1 minute, until the sauce has thickened somewhat. Take off fire.

3. Transfer to a serving dish and top with the rest of the red pepper strips and the rest of the basil leaves. Serve immediately, accompanied by steamed rice.

1 cup	vegetable oil	250 mL
4	Asian eggplants (1 lb/500 g), sliced irregularly in 2-inch/5-cm wedges	4
2 tbsp	vegetable oil	25 mL
1 tsp	chopped garlic	5 mL
2	fresh hot chilies, finely chopped	2
½	medium onion, roughly chopped	½
¼	medium red pepper, in thin strips	¼
2 tbsp	soya sauce	25 mL
1 tsp	sugar	5 mL
½ cup	water	125 mL
20	whole leaves fresh basil	20
½ tsp	cornstarch	2 mL
1 tbsp	water	15 mL
2½ cups	freshly steamed rice	625 mL

Serves 3-4.

Tao Pad Phed (Spicy Tofu with Watercress)

14 oz	fresh, pressed tofu	425 g
1	bunch fresh watercress	1
5 tbsp	vegetable oil	70 mL
1 tsp	chopped garlic	5 mL
2	fresh hot chilies, thinly chopped	2
4 oz	mushrooms, thickly sliced	125 g
3 tbsp	soya sauce	45 mL
½ tsp	sugar	2 mL
2 tbsp	water	25 mL
½ tsp	cornstarch	2 mL
1 tbsp	water	15 mL

Strips of red pepper
Fresh coriander leaves

2½ cups	freshly steamed rice	625 mL

Serve 3-4.

Tofu, the protein of choice for many vegetarians, is a favoured ingredient in Thailand, where vegetarianism is dictated (if not strictly followed) by the Buddhist religion. This recipe partners the versatile soybean derivative with slightly bitter watercress and sweet mushrooms in a mildly zesty sauce.

1. Slice tofu in ½-inch/1-cm thick, long strips. You'll get about 10 strips. Reserve.
2. Chop watercress in half horizontally. Reserve.
3. Heat oil in a wok (or large frying pan) on high heat until it is just about to smoke. Add reserved tofu strips and fry for about 3 minutes, turning them (carefully) 2 or 3 times, until the strips are golden brown all over. Do not overfry.
4. Make a well in the middle of the wok by pushing the tofu to the sides. Add garlic and chilies into the oil and stir-fry for 30 seconds. Immediately add reserved watercress and mushrooms and fold in once to start mixing with the tofu. Sprinkle soya sauce, sugar and water and gently stir-fry a few times to integrate the ingredients. Dissolve cornstarch in water, add to wok and stir-fry a few more times, being careful not to unduly break the tofu. Let cook another 30 seconds until the watercress has wilted and the sauce is bubbling. Take off fire.
5. Transfer to a serving dish and top with red pepper strips and coriander leaves. Serve immediately, accompanied by steamed rice.

Pad Het Hom (Stir-Fried Snow Peas with Shiitake Mushrooms)

Green, yellow, red and brown: a picture of vegetable happiness. This vibrantly coloured vegetable side course will complement any main dish. It takes no time at all to make, as long as one remembers to soak the mushrooms in advance.

1. Soak mushrooms in 2 cups/500mL hot water for 20 minutes. Drain and slice in thirds to obtain long ½-inch/1-cm wide pieces. Reserve.
2. Remove the strings of the snow peas. Reserve.
3. Heat oil in a wok (or large frying pan) on high heat until just about to smoke. Add garlic and stir-fry for 30 seconds. Add reserved mushroom slices and stir-fry for 30 seconds. Add reserved snow peas, red pepper and baby corn and stir in. Add soya sauce, water, sesame oil and salt and stir-fry for 2 minutes, until everything is shiny and slightly wilted. Dissolve cornstarch in water, add to wok and stir-fry for 1 more minute, until the sauce has thickened somewhat. Take off fire.
4. Transfer to a serving dish and sprinkle with black pepper. Top with red pepper strips and fresh coriander leaves. Serve immediately.

8	dried shiitake mushrooms	8
5 oz	snow peas	150 g
4 tbsp	vegetable oil	50 mL
1 tsp	chopped garlic	5 mL
½	medium red pepper, in ¼-inch/5-mm strips	½
5 oz	baby corn (canned)	150 g
2 tbsp	soya sauce	25 mL
½ cup	water	125 mL
½ tsp	sesame oil	2 mL
¼ tsp	salt	1 mL
½ tsp	cornstarch	2 mL
1 tbsp	water	15 mL

Pinch black pepper
Strips of red pepper
Fresh coriander leaves

Serves 4-5 as a vegetable course.

Tao Preow Waan
(Sweet and Sour Tofu)

½ tsp	tomato paste	2 mL
3 tbsp	rice (or white) vinegar	45 mL
1 tbsp	lime juice	15 mL
3 tsp	sugar	15 mL
4 tbsp	water	50 mL
4 tbsp	vegetable oil	50 mL
6 oz	fresh, pressed tofu, in ½-inch/1-cm cubes	165 g
1 tsp	chopped garlic	5 mL
½	small onion, roughly chopped	½
¼	medium red pepper, in ½-inch/1-cm squares	¼
½	small tomato, in ½-inch/1-cm pieces	½
1 inch	English cucumber, in ½-inch/1-cm wedges	2.5 cm
1 cup	pineapple, in ½-inch/1-cm pieces	250 mL
2 oz	mushrooms, quartered	60g

Here, another tofu dish, this time snugly absorbing the flavours of the famous sweet and sour sauce. The soft tofu contrasts pleasantly with the crunchy vegetables and lends itself to the strongly defined tastes of the sauce.

It is always advisable when planning any sweet and sour specialty to have another, somewhat less assertive dish on the table, as well as lots of rice. On its own, this combination of tart vegetables, sugar and vinegar can be overwhelming, but in alternate mouthfuls, it is wonderful.

1. Combine tomato paste, vinegar, lime juice, sugar and water in a small bowl and beat well to thoroughly mix. Reserve.
2. Heat oil in a wok (or large frying pan) on high heat until it is just about to smoke. Add tofu pieces and fry for 2 minutes, turning them carefully 2 or 3 times, until lightly golden brown all over.
3. Make a well in the middle of the wok by pushing the tofu to the sides. Add garlic to the oil and fry for 30 seconds. Immediately add onion, red pepper, tomato, cucumber, pineapple and mushrooms and fold in, stir-cooking for 30 seconds. Add soya sauce and salt and gently stir-cook for 1 minute.
4. Add reserved sauce from step #1, stir in and cook for 1 minute. Dissolve cornstarch in water, add along with green onion to wok and very gently stir-cook for 1 more minute, until the sauce has thickened somewhat.

5. Transfer to a deep serving dish and sprinkle with black pepper. Top with strips of red pepper and fresh coriander leaves and serve immediately with lots of steamed rice.

1 tbsp	soya sauce	15 mL
½ tsp	salt	2 mL
½ tsp	cornstarch	2mL
1 tbsp	water	15 mL
1	stem green onion, in 1-inch/2.5-cm pieces	1

Pinch black pepper
Strips of red pepper
Fresh coriander leaves

2½ cups	freshly steamed rice	625 mL

Serves 3-4.

Kang Ped Loochin Jai (Spicy Curry of Protein Tofu)

4	dried shiitake mushrooms	4
2 cups	unsweetened coconut milk	500 mL
2 tbsp	red curry paste	25 mL
2	lime leaves, torn into thirds	2
7 oz	*Mee Khing*, in ½-inch/1-cm pieces	200 g
1 tsp	sugar	5 mL
¼ tsp	salt	1 mL
2 oz	regular mushrooms, in quarters	60g
½	medium red pepper, in ¼-inch/5-mm strips	½
½	medium green pepper, in ¼-inch/5-mm strips	½
½ cup	water	125 mL
20	whole fresh basil leaves	20
1 tbsp	green peas (frozen)	15 mL

Additional red pepper strips

2½ cups	freshly steamed rice	625 mL

Serves 3-4.

Protein tofu, a spongy, adaptable substance made of wheat gluten, became popular in the early seventies, appearing as mock meat or seafood for alternate-lifestyler vegetarians who craved a meat substitute. In Asia it has been popular forever. Shaped like a thin sausage about 4 inches/10 cm long, it is known by its Chinese name, Mee Khing. *Wandee cooks it up in two versions, one hot and one even hotter. I start with this less hot recipe, which features it with the equally meaty shiitake mushrooms, alongside essential Thai condiments.*

1. Soak shiitake mushrooms in 2 cups/500 mL hot water for 20 minutes. Drain and slice in thirds to obtain long, ½ inch/1 cm wide pieces. Reserve.
2. Heat 1 cup/250 mL of the coconut milk in a wok (or large frying pan) on high heat until it boils. Add red curry paste and lime leaves and stir-cook for 2 minutes. Add *Mee Khing* and stir-fry for a few seconds. Add second cup of coconut milk and stir-cook for 1 minute. Add sugar, salt and the reserved shiitake mushroom pieces. Cook for 2-3 minutes, stirring occasionally, until the oil of the coconut milk rises to the top.
3. Add regular mushrooms, red and green pepper strips and water. Stir-cook for 1 minute. Add ⅔ of the basil leaves and the green peas. Stir-cook for 1 minute.
4. Transfer to a serving dish and top with the rest of the basil leaves and some red pepper strips. Serve immediately with steamed rice.

Pad Ped Nomai
(Protein Tofu and Bamboo Shoots in Hot Sauce)

The same Mee Khing *as the previous recipe is given the chili-hot treatment here in a combination that includes soothing bamboo shoots, crunchy red peppers and aromatic basil leaves. A perky, very satisfying vegetarian dish that loves its accompanying rice.*

4 tbsp	vegetable oil	50 mL
1 tsp	chopped garlic	5 mL
5	fresh hot chilies, thinly chopped	5
7 oz	*Mee Khing*, sliced on the bias, in ¼-inch/5-mm thick ovals	200 g
1 cup	bamboo shoot strips	250 mL
2 tbsp	soya sauce	25 mL
1 tsp	sugar	5 mL
½ cup	water	125 mL
2	lime leaves, torn in quarters	2
½ tsp	salt	2 mL
½	medium red pepper, in ¼-inch/5-mm strips	½
20	whole leaves fresh basil	20
1 tbsp	green peas (frozen)	15 mL
½ tsp	cornstarch	2 mL
1 tbsp	water	15 mL

Additional strips of red pepper

2½ cups	freshly steamed rice	625 mL

Serves 3-4.

1. Heat oil in a wok (or large frying pan) on high heat until it is just about to smoke. Add garlic and chilies and stir-fry for 30 seconds. Turn heat down to medium and add *Mee Khing* and bamboo shoots. Stir-fry for 1 minute.
2. Add soya sauce, sugar, water, lime leaves and salt and raise heat to maximum. Stir-fry for 1 minute. Add red pepper strips and ⅔ of the basil leaves. Stir-fry for 30 seconds. Add green peas and cornstarch dissolved in water. Stir-fry for 1 minute. Take off fire.
3. Transfer to a serving dish and top with the rest of the basil and some red pepper strips. Serve immediately with steamed rice.

Desserts

Klu Ay Bot Chi
(Sweet Banana with Coconut Milk)

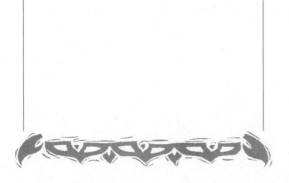

3	large bananas	3
3 cups	unsweetened coconut milk	750 mL
½ cup	sugar	125 mL
½ tsp	salt	2 mL

Serves 4-5.

(Leftovers can be refrigerated and rewarmed the next day.)

Cooked dessert in Thailand inevitably means either bananas or coconut milk, the two sweet ingredients that are in ample supply. Here's a recipe which combines them in a simple and unpretentious soup-like concoction that is bound to be a big (but messy) hit with children.

1. Choose bananas that are not 100% ripe. There should be some green highlights on the yellow skin. Peel and cut them on the bias, in 1-inch/2.5-cm thick, oval pieces. Reserve.
2. In a saucepan heat coconut milk, sugar and salt on high heat, stirring occasionally until the sugar is melted and the coconut milk is just beginning to reach a boil (about 2 minutes).
3. Add reserved banana pieces to the hot coconut milk and fold in. Lower heat to medium and let cook for 3 minutes. Do not stir. If stirred, the sauce will darken and the oil in the coconut milk will rise to the top. It is done when the banana has softened considerably. Take off fire. This dessert is now ready. It can be served immediately, or after it is cooled down (at which point it can also be refrigerated to be served cold).
4. To serve: place 3-4 banana pieces in each bowl and top with a good ladleful of the liquid.

Sweet Taro with Coconut Milk

A similar idea to the previous recipe, this one features the imported Chinese yam that we know from Chinese menus as taro. You'll need about half of a regular-sized taro for this recipe, and with the rest, you can make scrumptious french fries.

1. Peel taro, cut into ½-inch/1-cm rounds and slice the rounds into ½-inch/1-cm strips the size of fingers. Reserve.

2. In a saucepan heat coconut milk and water on high heat to boiling. Add reserved taro strips and reduce heat to medium. Cook, stirring infrequently for 20 minutes, until the taro has softened. Add sugar and salt and stir in. Continue cooking another 10 minutes. Reduce heat to minimum and simmer another 5-10 minutes, until the taro is soft and the liquid is richly bubbling. Take off fire and transfer to a deep bowl to start cooling off. This dessert is now ready, except for its topping. It can be served lukewarm, at room temperature, and also cold from the fridge if made in advance and chilled.

3. Meanwhile make the sauce: heat coconut milk in a saucepan on high heat for 1 minute, without stirring, until it reaches the boil. Immediately add salt and cornstarch dissolved in water. Reduce heat to medium, stir to mix the additions and cook for 1 minute, without letting it boil and without stirring, until it thickens somewhat. Take off fire and transfer to a serving bowl to allow it to cool off (it'll thicken further on its own to a thick cream consistency).

4. Pour about half of the coconut cream on top of the taro pudding and take it to the table for ladling into individual bowls. Serve the leftover coconut cream on the side.

18 oz	taro root	550 g
2 cups	unsweetened coconut milk	500 mL
1 cup	water	250 mL
½ cup	sugar	125 mL
½ tsp	salt	2 mL
	SAUCE:	
1 cup	unsweetened coconut milk	500 mL
½ tsp	salt	2 mL
¼ tsp	cornstarch	1 mL
1 tbsp	water	15 mL

Serves 4-6.

(Leftovers can be refrigerated and rewarmed the next day.)

Taro, an exotic potato-like tropical root vegetable, has a dark grey, hairy skin that can be peeled, with a bit of care, to reveal a speckled, cream-coloured flesh which is prized for its mealy, sweetish taste and its dense texture.

Saakoo Maprow
(Tapioca Pudding with Young Coconut)

1 can	young coconut in syrup (14 fl. oz/400 mL)	1 can
7 cups	water	1.75 L
1 cup	Thai tapioca	250 mL
1 cup	sugar	250 mL

SAUCE:		
2 cups	unsweetened coconut milk	500mL
1 tsp	salt	5 mL
½ tsp	cornstarch	2mL
1 tbsp	water	15 mL

Serves 5-7.

(Leftovers can be refrigerated and served the next day.)

An appreciation of tapioca, those pearly starchy grains of the cassava plant, is a prerequisite for the enjoyment of this dessert. Once over that hurdle, what we have is a smooth pudding with strips of crunchy young coconut (use canned: coconuts fresh from the palm tree are not particularly a Canadian staple), topped with a simple but irresistible coconut cream. This dessert is to be served cold and so it must be made in advance and refrigerated.

1. Drain young coconut, you'll have about 4 oz/125 g of the soft coconut flesh. Discard the syrup. Slice the coconut in ¼-inch/5-mm thick, long strips. Reserve.
2. Bring the water to a boil in a small soup-pot on high heat. Add tapioca and stir to prevent sticking as the mixture reaches the boil again. Reduce heat to medium, and let cook, stirring occasionally for 10 minutes, until the tapioca has become mostly translucent, except for the tiniest speck of solid white on each grain.
3. Add sugar and the reserved coconut strips. Stir, cooking for 2 minutes, just long enough to melt the sugar. Take off fire, and transfer to a deep bowl. The pudding at this time will be very watery, but as it cools down the tapioca will swell and absorb all the water. It is best to let it cool off at room temperature for an hour or so and then refrigerate it for another hour or two.

4. Meanwhile make the sauce. Heat coconut milk in a saucepan on high heat for about 2 minutes, without stirring, until it reaches the boil. Immediately add salt and cornstarch dissolved in water. Reduce heat to medium, stir to mix the additions and cook for 1 minute, without letting it boil and without stirring, until it thickens somewhat. Take off fire and transfer to a serving bowl. Allow it to cool off (it'll thicken further on its own to a thick cream consistency).

5. To serve: fill individual bowls with the cold tapioca pudding and nap with 2 tbsp/25 mL or more of the coconut sauce.

Khao Niow Mamuang (Sticky Rice Pudding with Mango)

2½ cups	Thai sticky rice	625 mL
2 cups	unsweetened coconut milk	500 mL
1 cup	sugar	250 mL
1 tsp	salt	5 mL
	SAUCE:	
1 cup	unsweetened coconut milk	250 mL
½ tsp	salt	2 mL
¼ tsp	cornstarch	1 mL
1 tbsp	water	15 mL

Slices of fresh mango
(or other fruit)

Serves 6-8.

(Leftovers can be refrigerated and rewarmed the next day.)

A far cry from the baby food we are used to, this one has a fabulous texture (derived from Thai sticky rice, whose grains remain individual though soft after steaming), and a deep coconuty taste. Its accompanying mango slices are a definite bonus, but can be substituted with slices of any other tropical fruit like pineapple and papaya if mangoes are unavailable. Mind you, a juicily ripe peach or pear in season can also serve admirably.

1. Soak the rice in plenty of warm water for at least 45 minutes (and up to 2-3 hours). Drain, wash and drain the rice again.
2. Steam the rice on medium-high heat for 25 minutes. (Wandee uses a Thai wicker steamer that fits on a saucepan.) A strainer lined with cheesecloth works well. Most importantly, the rice must be covered as it steams.
3. Meanwhile, mix 2 cups/500mL of the coconut milk with sugar and salt in a square dish (preferably glass). It requires a bit of stirring to incorporate the solids of the coconut milk and to dissolve the sugar. When the rice has finished steaming, add it on top of this sauce, flatten it out to cover the surface and cover the dish tightly for a 30-minute rest, during which the rice will absorb the sauce and finish its own cooking. Uncover and spoon it from the bottom up to transfer any leftover liquid to the top. Cover again and leave alone for 15 minutes or up to 2-3 hours.

4. Meanwhile make the sauce. Heat coconut milk in a saucepan on high heat for 1 minute, without stirring, until it reaches the boil. Immediately add salt and cornstarch dissolved in water. Reduce heat to medium, stir to mix the additions and cook for 1 minute, without letting it boil and without stirring, until it thickens somewhat. Take off fire and transfer to a serving bowl to allow it to cool off (it'll thicken further on its own to a thick cream consistency).

5. To serve, scoop out a 2-3-inch/5-7.5-cm square of the pudding onto individual plates. Nap generously with the coconut sauce and garnish with sliced mango.

For best results use Peacock Extra-Super Quality Thai sticky rice, which cooks soft and moist. Avoid the Japanese variety, which is too chewy.

Klu Ay Tod
(Thai Banana Fritters)

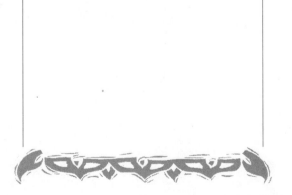

2 cups	self-rising flour	500 mL
1 tbsp	sugar	15 mL
1 tsp	salt	5 mL
1½ cups	water	375 mL
2	eggs, beaten	2
1 tsp	baking powder	5 mL
4	large bananas	4
4-6 cups	vegetable oil	1-1.5L
3-4 tbsp	honey	45-50 mL

Serves 4-6.

*(Leftovers can be refrigerated
and rewarmed,
but they won't be as good.)*

Having gone out of our way to eschew as much of the deep-fried recipes as possible (even eliminating the highly popular Mee Krob along the way), we close this book on Thai cooking with the cuisine's most popular dessert: deep-fried, breaded bananas, an international favourite. The recipe calls for lots of oil, but do not be alarmed; very little of it ends up in the fritters, especially if it reached exactly the right temperature prior to frying. The honey drizzle is merely the icing on this calorific affair that can be reserved for the most festive occasion, especially when children are involved.

1. Combine flour, sugar, salt and water and whisk in a work bowl until smooth. Add beaten eggs and baking powder and whisk to mix well. This batter can be made in advance and refrigerated until needed, or it can be used right away.
2. Choose bananas that are not 100% ripe (with a bit of green highlight on the yellow skin), peel them and cut into large (1-inch/2.5-cm) pieces. Add them to the batter and mix in to coat thoroughly.
3. Heat 4-6 cups/1-1.5 L vegetable oil in a large frying pan, to come at least 1 inch/2.5 cm up the sides, on high heat until hot, but not quite smoking. Test with a drop of batter. If it holds its shape and rises to the top, the oil is ready. Quickly spoon out coated banana pieces and add them to the oil, spacing them out somewhat so that they fry individually. Fry the first side for 1½-2 minutes, until golden, Turn heat down to medium-high, and flip the fritters over to fry the second side,

frying 1½-2 minutes until also golden. Turn heat down to medium-low and continue flipping the fritters for another 2 minutes, to crisp them, and have them turn rosy brown all over. Scoop them out of the oil with a slotted spoon and transfer them to a serving dish.

4. Immediately drizzle them generously and evenly with honey and serve as soon as possible while still warm.

Index